THE

BRAIN
POWER
CLASSROOM

"The Brain Power program assists me as a leader to create a school environment that is positive and collaborative. The dynamic activities that this program teaches can transform the way leaders, teachers, and students interact with each other to build trust and meaningful relationships so that the magic of teaching and learning can happen effectively."

Deborah Sanabria
Principal, JHS 162X

"The Brain Power program is helping my teachers and students to manage their stress, increase concentration, and develop the internal efficacy to create peaceful ways to interact with themselves and others."

Reva Gluck Schneider
Principal, PS 144Q

"The Brain Power program is a necessary tool to align positive energy in daily life. It fosters building healthy minds, bodies, and citizens of the earth for a better tomorrow. Brain Power rocks!"

Harriet Diaz
Principal, IS 192Q

"The most direct impact I see is the change in the attitude of our teachers. We are more collaborative and use Brain Power language to support each other. We are also able to support ourselves. When we make a mistake, we keep a more positive frame of mind. This positive, confident mindset is transferring to the students, who thoroughly enjoy and look forward to all our Brain Power activities."

Bernice Acevedo
Principal, Lenox Elementary
Baldwin, NY

"The Brain Power program provides great tools in which students can exercise their ability to feel confident, positive, and healthy. Our schools are grateful for taking part in the Brain Power program and working alongside such an amazing group of leaders."

Wendy Soto
Guidance Counselor, MS 29

"I have found the Brain Power program to be a truly transformational system for my staff and students. Brain Power has facilitated a sense of collaborative teamwork that has improved relationships and promoted the family atmosphere essential to teacher and student success. Within this positive environment, group decision making becomes easier, as people are more open to new ideas. We look forward to implementing the Brain Power programs at PS 1X as we continue to make great gains in our academic and social progress."

Jorge Perdomo
Principal, PS 1X

THE
BRAIN
POWER
CLASSROOM

10 Essentials
for Focus, Mindfulness,
and Emotional Wellness

DAVE BEAL

BEST
LIFE
MEDIA

BEST
LIFE
MEDIA

459 N. Gilbert Rd, Suite C-210
Gilbert, AZ 85234
www.bestlifemedia.com
(480) 926-2480

First paperback edition: November 2016
Library of Congress Control Number: 2016955586
ISBN-13: 978-1-935127-93-2

Cover and interior design by Kiryl Lysenka

Dedicated to Dawn Marie, my beautiful life partner, and our amazing son Julian, who inspire me each day to be a Power Brain.

TABLE OF CONTENTS

This Book Will Inspire and Equip You to Empower Your Students

What can teachers do to inspire students to learn—to make them want to learn? Dave Beal's book, *The Brain Power Classroom*, addresses this issue by presenting a teaching program suitable for all grade levels.

In the Introduction, the author explains that he began a career in teaching because he wanted to make a difference; he wanted to empower young people to reach their full potential. Instead, he found himself ill-equipped to navigate the challenges he faced when working with students. Essentially, this book is the story of how Dave turned negatives into positives through the use of mindfulness techniques.

I worked with this fine educator during his presentations at Molloy College's Phi Delta Kappa International workshops. His presentation drew over 150 participants who wanted to learn about having a "Power Brain." Later, when I gave a keynote address at a conference he had arranged, I was able to see his dedication. As he shared his experiences, he assisted others in creating classrooms where learning is observable and palpable. But, his work doesn't just serve classroom educators—it's for parents, students—anyone interested in improving their concentration, material retention, cooperation, and learning ability.

The classroom practices he describes engage the learner and create a welcoming classroom atmosphere. In Part 1 of the book, there are seven chapters, starting with a definition of the Brain Power Classroom and concluding with tips for managing the classroom through collaboration. Part 2 explains the ten "essentials" of the Brain Power Classroom. Basically, Dave helps teachers to instill the skills of self-reliance and self-empowerment. These practices include establishing high levels of student engagement, developing passion and motivation in teachers, and nurturing students' intrinsic motivation to learn. The book includes examples of peer teaching and other activities to engage teachers and student learners. Everything is made clear through numerous tables, illustrations, comments from student learners, and quotes from educational experts.

WHEN WE FEEL GOOD, WE DO GOOD

While reading Dave's book, I found an underlying premise with which I definitely concur. This point of agreement appears in the book's first section, and I would interpret and synthsize this message as being: "Ultimately, if you enjoy the environment you're in . . . then you're open to learning." *The Brain Power Classroom* offers means to make the learning environment enjoyable, agreeable, comfortable, and equitable for all those present.

A portion of the book's content also covers the neuroscience related to the Power Brain. It examines how emotions, memory, physical health, creativity, and cognition all play into the learning process. It also describes the theories behind attention and multiple intelligences. Scientific information about the brain, such as the explanation of neuroplasticity, is presented simply and directly, so as to be easily digested and put into practice. Illustrations are also an enjoyable and engaging part of this book, which helps make information about the brain easy to understand.

At one point, the book quotes Haim Ginott's statement about the teacher being the decisive element in the classroom. *The Brain Power Classroom* takes that idea a step further, however, by insisting that students are also a decisive factor, not just the teacher. As students learn about mindfulness and about being a Power Brain, they learn to take on more responsibility for their own learning process. As the book's author explains, "When we feel good, we do good." To help educators create a positive atmosphere, the book gives advice for managing student and/or personal stress and for maintaining peace when conflicting emotions arise.

One of my favorite chapters is titled "Classroom Management: From Control to Collaboration." As Dave states in the beginning of the book, the idea of teacher control is a serious issue these days. In this chapter, he explains that less control is actually necessary to create happy classroom students. The goal is to create an educational setting that is harmonious for all present, and teacher modeling of this is important, too, according to Beal.

Part 2 of this book presents specific activities, as well as extensions and modifications of them. Dave explains the goals and benefits of practicing them, and provides clear objectives for each exercise and for each portion of the book. The chapters are configured to bring forth an "I can do this" attitude in the reader. Finally, the book encourages readers to realize the important mission of education: "to help student learners realize their own potential and to help them identify the reasons why they are doing classroom work."

Close to the end of this "tour de force" book, there are two more concepts I found important. The first is Ilchi Lee's concept of being "Earth Citizens," a philosophy that encourages us to live united as one people. As Earth Citizens, we must learn to live harmoniously with ourselves and others. This is a book that gives people real hope that that goal is both achievable and practical.

The second concept is summed up by a quote from Albert Einstein: "Imagination is more important than knowledge." In my opinion, this book has an abundance of both imagination and knowledge, both in the way it is presented and in the educational activities it presents! I hope you will enjoy reading it, and that it inspires you to be the best you can be, both for those you teach in the classroom and for those you encounter on your life's journey.

Marjorie S. Schiering, Ph.D.
Professor of Education at Molloy College, NY
Author of *Teaching Creative and Critical Thinking* and *Learning and Teaching Creative Cognition*

How Brain Education Changed My Classroom and My Life

In May 2004, I was wrapping up my second year of teaching fifth grade at Public School 375 in Crown Heights, Brooklyn. At that time, the school was the fifth lowest performing school in New York City. I had come to the school in 2002 as a Teaching Fellow, eager to make a difference. Through the Teaching Fellows program, I received an outstanding graduate degree in education from Pace University; however, I didn't know how ill-equipped I was to navigate the challenges of having my own classroom. Just two years into my career, I began suffering from headaches, insomnia, and chest pain, even though I exercised regularly and ate well. I had become a teacher because I wanted to really change the world, to empower students to grow into their potential. Instead, I felt more like I was on the brink of being just another burned-out inner-city school teacher. I was losing hope.

Public School 375 was intense. Five security guards and two deans roamed the building that housed one thousand students, from Pre-K through Grade 8. Ninety-nine percent of the students received free or reduced lunch, and the vast majority scored Level 1 (significantly below grade level) on the New York

State math and English language arts assessments. During my three years at the school, three principals had come and gone, and the overall atmosphere felt tense and unstable.

Students routinely ran through the halls, cursing, fighting, and ripping down bulletin boards. Drugs and weapon raids were common. As a Grade 5 teacher, I myself felt like a police officer on many occasions, breaking up hallway fights, trying to shield my students from the often profane example being set for them by the middle schoolers. Many of my colleagues also absorbed the stress of the environment. When I first took the job, the assistant principal warned me not to go into the teacher's lounge. I thought it was an odd request, but when I did finally go, I heard my colleagues complaining loudly about the kids, the principal, the parents, the Department of Education, the mayor, and so on. I vowed to myself I would never become like that.

I was able to get through my first two years of teaching on passion, adrenaline, and coffee. *Lots* of coffee. I really loved my students, and I would stay up late creating hip hop songs to teach social studies or masterminding cool field trips to technology museums or off-Broadway shows. I volunteered to facilitate our afterschool hip hop club and founded our school's Peer Mediation and Conflict Resolution program. I really cared about my job, and I truly wanted to make a difference. And at times, I felt like I was. I had many triumphant moments where students had academic or social breakthroughs, and I learned so much from them. But I also had far too many instances of utter frustration over lack of student progress and, above all, challenging student behavior.

BECAUSE . . . I AM THE TEACHER

The majority of our students, teachers, and administrators had West Indian roots—beautiful, rich, and diverse cultures. One commonality of these cultures, whether from Jamaica, Trinidad, Barbados, or Grenada, is a cultural respect for, and adherence to, authority, particularly teachers. During parent-teacher conferences, it was common for the parents of my students—particularly the students prone to getting into trouble—to make it clear to their child that they should listen to everything I said because he is the teacher. This air of authority permeated the culture of my school, and I quickly got the message that our students "needed" a top-down, sharp idea of discipline. Eager to please and prove myself as capable, I took great pride in making my class stand up straight in two lines in the hallway without making a sound (if I heard a noise we would often go back and try walking again until we were perfectly silent). I instituted a "stick chart" of rewards and consequences. If I placed a green Popsicle stick in your name pocket it was an initial warning. A yellow stick meant "proceed with caution." A red stick meant a loss of privileges (computer time, silent lunch, etc.). A purple stick was a note home and lunch detention the following day.

I, like all the teachers in the school, routinely raised my voice in frustration and was not above berating a child who was "out of line." As the only male teacher on the grade, I also became an "enforcer" to discipline boys who acted out in other classes. I took pride in having my students sit up straight and show me respect . . . because I was the teacher.

Deep down, this approach didn't feel right. I became a teacher to create a more positive world and yelling at children just didn't seem like a logical path to get there. One of my heroes has always been the amazing peace activist Mahatma Gandhi, who famously said, "Be the change you wish to see in the world." In order to help my students solve interpersonal conflicts, I had become trained in Peer Mediation and Conflict Resolution, and I trained all my students in respectful and proactive communication. However, within my school's prevailing control paradigm, it was acceptable for me, as the teacher, to succumb to my emotions and openly yell and criticize my students. The hypocrisy became too much for me to rationalize.

WHAT I LEARNED FROM RACHEL

Despite all of this, I was given a proficient rating, the highest rating possible, by my assistant principal, and my reward for making it through my first two years "successfully" was the honor of teaching Class 506. This was the lowest-performing class in the grade, conveniently filled with all the boys that my fourth grade colleagues couldn't handle the year before. I was convinced that my fifth grade colleagues, all of whom out-ranked me in seniority, had conspired against me over the summer by assembling this group, but, nonetheless, I was ready. Or so I thought.

See, over the summer, I had taken up yoga, impressed by my wife Dawn's amazing vibrancy after her taking yoga classes, and started to feel more energized and more in control of my emotions. I read several books on integrating positive communication in the classroom and couldn't wait to try it out. I was ready for a new start. To begin, I tried implementing "circle time" where the kids and I would take off our shoes and talk about our feelings. Unfortunately, on the first day of school with Class 506, "circle time" turned into "let's insult each other and wrestle on the floor time." I somehow managed to survive until sixth period, when I asked the students to line up to go to their elective class. And then came Rachel. She was a petite little girl with bright eyes behind her thick glasses. Rachel, who I later found out was living in foster care, decided she did not want to line up with the class. When I ordered her to get in line she informed me that I wasn't her father and employed a variety of colorful language to communicate the fact that she didn't have to listen to anything I said. If you've never been cursed out by a sixty-five-pound fifth grade girl in front of twenty-nine other fifth graders, I highly recommend it. It was actually a very awakening moment for me. In that moment of frustration and embarrassment, I realized a simple truth: I could not make anyone do anything. Something had to change.

BRAIN POWER TO THE RESCUE

After the rocky start to the year, I alternated between trying to be nurturing and fun and slipping back into my authoritarian default mode. My students in 506 faced myriad obstacles to their success. Some of these were external: abusive home situations, lack of clean clothes to wear to school, family members being arrested or killed, etc. They also had many internalized challenges, namely in the form of limiting beliefs about themselves. Many thought they were stupid, that school was a waste of time, or that they needed to constantly be tough and keep up their guard to protect themselves. While I could empathize and understand where these attitudes came from, I felt like none of my graduate classes or prior experiences helped me create the breakthroughs these kids needed. As a result, it was normal for my students to channel this frustration into two or three fights each day in the cafeteria, schoolyard, or even in my classroom.

One day I heard of a Brain Power weekend workshop being offered at the local Body & Brain Center where I was taking yoga and Tai Chi classes. It seemed like this was what I was looking for: physical and mental exercises to bring into the classroom to promote focus, confidence, and emotional wellness. Without mentioning it to my principal, whom I was sure wouldn't approve of this holistic approach, I paid my own way and took the training.

I had been to tons of Professional Development trainings in my three years in education, but this workshop was totally different. Instead of just looking at presentations or analyzing data, from the outset, we were up and moving, enthusiastically participating in the exercises we were to bring to our students. Within twenty minutes, I forgot all about my problems and completely locked in to the activities.

The instructor, Nora, was positive, passionate, and powerful. Whereas many teacher workshops go through the motions, explaining concepts and theories, Nora really wanted us to feel the benefits these exercises could have on our own mental and emotional state. "You can't give what you don't have," Nora told us. "Knowing what to do is not enough. You must take action if you want to make a change." As the workshop got progressively deeper and the activities became more difficult, Nora would remind us with a smile, "Your brain loves challenges!" and "Trust your brain—you can do it!" She was like a gentle drill sergeant, motivating us with her positive mindset, but not allowing us to do anything less than our best.

In two short days, I felt completely refreshed. The physical exercises—push-ups, stretching, energy accumulation Tai Chi postures—felt great; the meditation and emotional release activities helped me let go of tension I didn't even realize I was holding inside; the mental flexibility training challenged my brain in ways that enabled me to actually feel the new synapses forming. Above all, the workshop reminded me why I became a teacher. I wanted to bring this feeling of health, happiness, and empowerment to my students. I wanted to change their lives.

When Monday morning rolled around, I was determined to implement what I had learned. I started by teaching the class a set of moves called the Power Brain Dance. Now, this partner activity is super fun and super silly, so I knew many of my tougher kids wouldn't take to it, but I remembered what Nora had told me: "As the saying goes, the definition of insanity is trying the same thing over and over and expecting a different result. If you want to change the outcome, you can't be afraid to change your approach. No action, no creation." As I introduced the Power Brain Dance, complete with high-fives and do-si-do's, more than half the class laughed at me and refused to participate, but the kids who did it felt great.

Next I showed them the Pinky-Thumb Brain Versatilizing exercise. It was tough and many of them gave up, but I encouraged them to "trust your brain" and remember that "mistakes are okay." We laughed together as we tried to figure it out, and I noticed the mood starting to get lighter. Each day, I would set aside a couple of minutes in the morning and afternoon to introduce some new Brain Power exercises, and the class started to really get into it. All but one student that is.

Kwame was a charming, quick-witted, and short-tempered boy from Trinidad, and he was the coolest kid in my class. Even though many of the other boys were a head taller than Kwame, everyone showed him respect. When we would start Brain Power, he would simply sit down. He occasionally made jokes under his breath about the kids as they did the exercises, which made some of them feel self-conscious. I tried each day to gently encourage Kwame to participate, but he was steadfast in his resistance.

After a week or so, Kwame came up to me in the afternoon when the students were finishing independent Social Studies work. "Mr. Beal, the schedule says we got Brain Power now. Are we gonna do Brain Power today?" Surprised, I replied with a smile, "Kwame, I thought you didn't like Brain Power." He quickly quipped, "I'm not saying I like it, I'm just asking are we gonna do it." "Well," I replied, "I don't know, Kwame. We're a little behind schedule. If we don't finish this Social Studies lesson soon, we won't have time." "Alright," he said. He walked back slowly toward his seat, and, when he thought I wasn't looking, he whispered to everyone nearby, "Hurry up, y'all! Let's finish."

I did my best to hide my excitement, but made sure we made time for some Brain Power exercises, and Kwame participated in each one. While I didn't say anything about it to the whole class, I could tell everyone was relieved that Kwame chose to join. At the end of the day, I quietly told him, "Hey, Kwame, thanks for doing Brain Power today. I'm really glad you joined us." Although he tried hard to shrug off my praise, I saw his chest puff out a little bit.

Once Kwame took to the activities, Brain Power switched gears, and the changes were impossible to ignore. We went from a class that regularly saw two or three fights a day to two weeks of relative peace and positivity. And then . . . Terrell and Devante bumped into each other on their way back from lunch, inciting a cursing and pushing match. Before the fists went up, I broke in, commanding, "Push-ups!"

Push-ups had become a daily routine in my class, and the kids loved it. While we integrated push-ups into the curriculum, using them as data in math lessons to teach graphing and calculation, my students had learned that push-ups were also a great way to release emotional tension. Without a grumble, the boys hit the floor, giving each other death stares. Full of adrenaline and cortisol, Terrell and Devante began their push-ups at a rapid pace as their classmates excitedly counted and cheered for them.

As eleven-year-old boys, the most push-ups they had ever done at once was about fifteen, but fueled by their emotions and hormones, each boy kept going, "twenty-six, twenty-seven . . ." Their breathing was heavy and their arms trembled . . . "thirty-nine, forty . . ." I could tell they were almost out of juice, but it was clear they were locked in an epic competition, both determined to win. By the time the class yelled "fifty," both boys collapsed to the floor, exhausted. Then, without saying a word, they stood up and hugged each other. (OK, so it wasn't a full hug, but they gave each other a cool one-armed "dap" hug.)

Eventually, they both came to their senses and jumped away from each other, worried that the other still had intentions to fight, but neither boy did. The anger was totally gone, and all that was left was respect and friendship. I was dumbfounded. Before my Brain Power workshop, I would have broken up that fight, separated the boys and most likely lectured them with enlightened statements like, "You know better than this!" and, "Why did you do that?!" I would have made them use Conflict Resolution to talk out the problem under threat of being referred to the principal.

But this time, the boys were my teacher. In one minute, they had released the anger and solved the problem. In that brief moment, I thought back to how much class time my students and I had wasted with interpersonal disputes or emotional outbursts. I thought of the harsh statistics facing my African American boys in this neighborhood, and how what I had just witnessed—young people of color authentically solving their conflicts peacefully and proactively—was a huge part of what inspired me to become a teacher in the first place. Terrell and Devante touched my heart. And they inspired me even more to use Brain Power to help all my students manage their emotions.

A WHOLE NEW CLASS

With only three months left of school, my class had become immune to fighting, just in time for the state tests in April. At the beginning of the year, I had presented the kids with the practice test. Defiant, some had shredded the sheets of paper, saying, "Why should I bother taking this if I'm going to fail anyway?"

Now, I watched the same students practice an "Energy Ball" visualization I had taught them, imagining their success on their "BrainScreens." As a result, which seemed an impossibility at the beginning of the year, 100 percent of my students sat for the exam. Did the kids instantly go from a level 1 to a level 4? No, but the important thing is that they did their best, and that was all I could ask. My classroom was no longer a losing battle; instead, it was a place where kids could take refuge from the chaotic outside world and embrace the positive relationships we had created as a class.

When I first started teaching Brain Power, I would close my doors for fear that my principal would chastise me for taking precious time away from test prep. After a month of training, however, my principal sought me out and said, "Mr. Beal, what's going on? Your kids aren't in my office anymore, and they aren't giving the school aides a hard time in the cafeteria. They're not fighting out in the yard. They're respectful. Something's up."

That's when I invited her in to my classroom for a demonstration. The principal was blown away by the exercises, which ranged from physical to meditative to team building. She green-lighted the program for more of the staff, allocating funds to pay for our Brain Power certifications. Over the next three months, I finally got a glimpse of what teaching was really about and what it should feel like. My students and I both started to feel our true potential.

After Class 506, I taught two more years, creating a successful school-wide Brain Power program in my new school, Bayview Avenue Elementary in Freeport, Long Island. But ever since I had witnessed Terrell and Devante give each other dap, I knew that my dream was to share Brain Power with every child in the U.S. In 2007, I made the teary-eyed decision to leave the classroom to work full-time as a Brain Power trainer. Since then, I have had the honor of working with over four hundred schools, more than 12,000 teachers, and 50,000 students. I've been able to lead empowerment camps around the country for kids and adults and give lectures and workshops on four continents. As of this writing, our program is being used by ten districts within the

New York City school system, and the Chancellor of New York City schools has publicly praised our program and supports our efforts to spread Brain Power to all 1.1 million children in New York City. But this is just the beginning.

THE ROOT OF THE BRAIN POWER PROGRAM

Ilchi Lee and his Brain Education, the basis for the Brain Power program, is a constant inspiration for me. A true believer in the power of each person to change themselves and the world around them, Ilchi Lee has sought to empower individuals to live according to their highest ideals and dreams. He identifies the human brain as the source of this ability, and considers its development and actualization the most critical aspect of human progress. Brain Education, a collection of systemized mind-body training programs that help to unlock the brain's true potential, is the primary fruit of his thirty-six years of endeavor.

The Brain Power program was born from over ten years of applying Brain Education in the U.S. school system. It is an innovative educational approach that combines progressive research from the fields of neuroscience and education with traditional Eastern practices for energy development and mindfulness. You will grab the very essence of the Brain Power program from this book.

Brain Education has also been applied to other environments, and has now become an academic discipline in its own right. A research institute and graduate university have been established in Ilchi Lee's home country of South Korea to facilitate more specialized research, teaching, and dissemination of Brain Education. The national government of South Korea recognizes Brain Education trainers as a specialized profession. Furthermore, through the Benjamin School for Character Education, an innovative gap year program, high school students are discov-

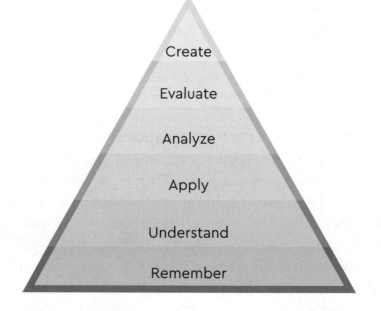

BLOOM'S TAXONOMY

ering their passion and self-worth by using Brain Education to successfully complete "Dream Projects" that benefit their community. When I visit South Korea and talk with the young Brain Education student leaders there, I feel inspired and full of hope at what we can create for our world.

HOW TO USE THIS BOOK

The purpose of this book is to provide educators with practical strategies, activities, exercises, and guidelines that help create a Brain Power Classroom. While I find the theory behind the concepts in this book to be fascinating, the scope of this book is meant to be practical and easily accessible. In consideration of Bloom's Taxonomy, the objective of this book is not merely to understand, analyze, or evaluate what a Brain Power Classroom

BRAIN POWER 10

looks like or how it benefits student development. Rather, the objective is to help you *create* a Brain Power Classroom and reap its benefits right now.

Part 1 of this book provides basic information about the brain and its functions as well as the philosophical framework of Brain Education.

Part 2 is comprised of the ten Essentials of Brain Power—aspects critical to the development of the whole child that the Brain Power program addresses with specific individual and group exercises. Each Essential—team building, physical health, focus, mindfulness, memory, emotional wellness, confidence, creativity, character, and citizenship—is accompanied by three engaging activities, benefits boxes, advice on when to use each activity, and research information that sheds light on the purpose of the Essential and how it leads to teaching students to use their whole brain.

Throughout both parts of the book, I will share my own experiences with using Brain Education and introduce you to some of the most challenging, lively, and rewarding scenarios I have come across as I personally transitioned from teaching in a classroom to participating in a Brain Power Classroom.

I HAVE A DREAM

Just as Martin Luther King Jr. implored a nation to dream of a brighter future for humanity, Ilchi Lee's Brain Education program holds the power of the dream as a major key to harnessing our brain power.

My dream is to share Brain Power with every child, parent, and teacher in the United States. Like Dr. King, Ilchi Lee, and many other visionary leaders, I believe wholeheartedly in the purity of the human spirit, and I know Brain Power to be a powerful system through which we can grow strong, passionate, creative leaders who will transform our world.

I thank you for reading my story, and I sincerely hope that you will find this book to be both inspirational and practically helpful in your journey to become the best teacher and person you can be.

Dave Beal
East Meadow, NY
November 2016

The Brain Power Rules

CHAPTER 1

What Is a Brain Power Classroom?

Tell me, and I forget. Teach me, and I remember. Involve me, and I learn.
– Benjamin Franklin

Classroom (noun) a room, typically in a school, in which a class of students is taught.

Brain Power Classroom (noun) 1. a harmonious, collaborative learning environment co-created by healthy, happy, and engaged students along with their teachers; an environment that utilizes authentic academic rigor, character development, and social-emotional wellness as the foundation for helping members of the class draw out their innate brilliance and cultivate their brightest life purpose; 2. an awesome place to learn and teach.

The concepts and tools you will discover in this book will help you transform your classroom into a Brain Power Classroom. But what exactly does that mean? A Brain Power Classroom is one that possesses the following elements:

- High levels of student engagement
- Passionate, motivated teachers

- Intrinsic motivation to learn
- Positive discipline based on compassion and mutual respect
- Peer teaching and authentic student leadership
- Academic rigor that includes creative assessments, reflecting diverse learning styles and multiple intelligences
- Self-regulation of emotions and physical energy levels
- Routines that foster harmonious collaboration
- Love and laughter
- Healthy, happy humans

All of the above can be achieved by focusing on the following four themes:

1. STUDENT ENGAGEMENT

Research shows that time-on-task, motivation, and student interest play a huge role in learning. Furthermore, activating valuable non-cognitive skills such as passion, curiosity, and positive attitude helps increase academic achievement. In addition, creating relevant tasks that provide students with an authentic voice within a collaborative, democratic atmosphere helps maximize engagement. In this book, you will learn a number of strategies and activities to optimize student engagement in all its forms: intellectual, emotional, behavioral, physical, and social.

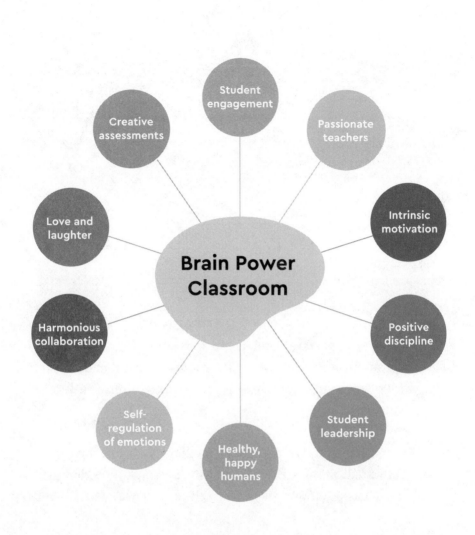

BRAIN POWER CLASSROOM

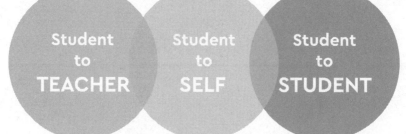

POSITIVE CLASSROOM RELATIONSHIPS

2. POSITIVE CLASSROOM RELATIONSHIPS

Positive atmospheres and positive relationships are interdependent. In a Brain Power Classroom, students and teachers work together to create three positive types of relationships on a daily basis.

- **Student to Self:** Through meditation, breathing, and visualization, students engage in personal reflection to develop self-awareness and self-confidence.

- **Student to Teacher:** Through engaging games and exercises, students interact positively with teachers while co-creating an atmosphere of mutual trust and respect.

- **Student to Student:** Team building activities, small group discussion, and authentic peer teaching creates a respectful, collaborative environment.

3. HOLISTIC HEALTH

Brain Education recognizes the connection between physical, emotional, and cognitive development, and this book provides easy-to-follow classroom activities to create healthy integration of all three aspects of life.

4. POSITIVE PSYCHOLOGY

Through the Brain Power phrases, the Brain Declaration, and a variety of empowering language and lessons, Brain Power gives students authentic practice in creating and sustaining a positive mindset.

Have Fun!

Research demonstrates that students who enjoy school are more successful academically. To create a fun, challenging environment, this book offers many exercises, games, and partner activities that promote a nurturing and supportive atmosphere. The fact that teachers engage in the activities along with their students also enhances the teacher-to-student relationship. Have fun playing Brain Power games with your students!

CHAPTER 2

Brain Science 101

The human brain has one hundred billion neurons, each neuron connected to 10,000 other neurons. Sitting on your shoulders is the most complicated object in the known universe.
– Michio Kaku

While you certainly don't have to be a neuroscientist to appreciate the positive impact of Brain Power, some background on the brain can help you use Brain Power more effectively in your classroom.

KEY NEUROSCIENCE CONCEPTS

First, there are key neuroscience concepts that are relevant to Brain Power and into which all the activities in each of the ten Essentials in Part 2 of this book aim to tap.

- **Brain Wave Optimization:** Having their brain waves at an alpha frequency helps students improve focus, memory, and emotional regulation. Mindfulness training helps students balance their brain waves and create alpha waves when they need sustained focus.

- **Neuroplasticity:** The brain's ability to create new synapses and change in structure and chemistry. In short, the brain is not static; it can change.
- **Neurogenesis:** The brain's ability to grow new cells at any age. Neuroscience teaches us that exercise and brain training can accelerate this process.
- **Emotions and Learning:** The fact that emotions can enhance or impair learning.
- **Learning and Memory:** Teaching strategies that enhance student engagement, emphasize relevancy, and stimulate multiple learning styles strengthen long-term memory and boost comprehension of content.
- **Physical Health and Learning:** Exercise, breathing, and hydration have a significant impact on learning.
- **The Arts and Cognition:** The visual and performing arts provide a host of benefits for the brain, including enhancing attention and memory.
- **Attention and Learning:** Concentration can be strengthened by enhancing one's environment and through specific brain training.
- **Multiple Intelligence Theory:** Addressing students' unique learning styles through multiple modalities improves their chances to learn successfully.

NEURONS AND SYNAPSES

Human beings have an estimated one hundred billion brain cells, or neurons, which form a sophisticated network. These neurons connect with one another through synapses—tiny gaps between neurons that enable the cells to communicate through electrochemical impulses. Each neuron can communicate with

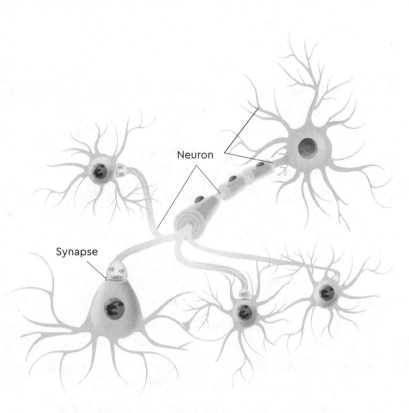

NEURONS AND SYNAPSES

up to 50,000 other neurons, which means we have the potential for hundreds of trillions of possible connections. To put this in astonishing perspective, the number of possible neural connections in our brain is equivalent to the number of stars that would fill 1,500 Milky Way galaxies.

We are born with all of the neurons we need throughout our lives, and when we are young children, synapses form at a rapid rate. As we head into our teenage years, these connections get pruned so that our brains work more efficiently and with greater sophistication.

NEUROPLASTICITY

If the name of the game is creating more neural connections, how do we do it? The answer is simple and inspiring: by doing new things that challenge our brain.

Neuroplasticity is the process by which the brain's neural synapses and pathways are altered as an effect of environmental, behavioral, and/or neural changes. In his seminal work, *The Brain That Changes Itself*, Norman Doidge, M.D. illustrates this process by detailing inspiring stories of stroke and traumatic brain injury victims who were able to use brain training to recover previously inconceivable amounts of cognitive function.

The ability the brain has to heal itself has huge implications for the way we can help shape and mold our students' young brains. Brain Versatilizing exercises, such as those found in Essential 3: Focus in Part 2 of this book, are designed to help students create new neural pathways and build stronger neural networks by challenging their brains with novel tasks. We can literally help our students build a stronger brain. This is why one of the basic Brain Power phrases is, "My brain loves challenges."

THE RIGHT AND LEFT BRAIN

We've all heard about the two halves of our brains. Some of us may even identify ourselves as being a "right brain" or "left brain" person. In a broad sense, the left hemisphere is more analytically inclined; it is the primary region responsible for verbal language and mathematical processes. The right hemisphere functions in a more abstract way, as the center for non-verbal thought and visual-spatial perceptions. A properly functioning brain requires intimate and coordinated interaction between both sides of the brain, made possible by a bridge of nerve fibers called the corpus callosum, which connects the two hemispheres.

Brain Power training, including several of the activities in

Essential 1: Team Building, Essential 2: Physical Health, and Essential 3: Focus, help connect the left and right hemispheres. In so doing, Brain Power helps students create a more flexible brain while developing and coordinating creative and logical intelligence, which promotes logical thinkers and creative problem solvers.

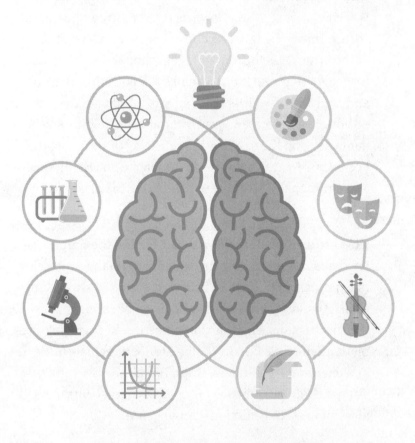

THE RIGHT AND LEFT BRAIN

THREE LAYERS OF THE BRAIN

Our brain can be divided into three main layers that reflect the three fundamental aspects of our existence: physical, social/emotional, and cognitive. These layers are thought to have evolved over time, beginning with our most basic physical drives and culminating with conceptual and analytical thinking.

- **The Neocortex:** At the top of the evolutionary ladder is the neocortex. Also known as the cerebrum or cerebral cortex, this is the most recently evolved and largest part of the brain. It is the seat of higher thought, writing, and language. It grants human beings the powers of reason and analysis, as well as the ability to anticipate the future. As educators, we spend much of our time helping students develop the executive functioning of the neocortex; however, research shows that students who are physically and emotionally healthy are better able to harness the neocortex's immense power.

- **The Limbic System:** Further inside lies the limbic system, which controls learning and memory, the expression of emotions, and the linking of past events to strong emotions. An older part of the brain, it can be thought of as the source of our emotional intelligence. Recognizing the plethora of research correlating academic achievement and emotional well-being, Brain Power offers a variety of strategies, games, and exercises to encourage intrapersonal awareness and emotional intelligence.

- **The Brain Stem:** At the deepest and oldest level is the reptilian brain. The brain stem controls basic life functions, including digestion, respiration, circulation, and "fight or flight" stress responses, working independently of the conscious brain. Through a variety of

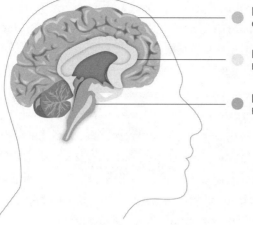

Neocortex
Cognitive Health

Limbic System
Emotional Health

Brain Stem
Physical Health

THREE LAYERS OF THE BRAIN

physical exercises, Brain Power helps to optimize the brain stem's functioning and improve the connection between the body and brain.

A Power Brain is one that engages all three layers of the brain so they work at an optimal level and in a coordinated fashion. Brain Power exercises simultaneously involve the cognitive, emotional, and physical aspects of our being, integrating them to give students greater control, which allows them to use their full potential effectively for their goals. By stimulating the whole brain, Brain Power training seamlessly addresses the needs of the whole child.

BRAIN ACTIVITY AND BRAIN WAVES

There are four types of brain waves, which reflect the electrical activity of the brain.

- **Beta waves:** This is the brain's rhythm in its normal, wakeful state. Beta waves are associated with thinking, conscious problem solving, and active attention to the outside world. You are most likely in the beta state while you are reading this book.

- **Alpha waves:** When in a state of relaxation, the brain's activity slows from the rapid patterns of beta to the gentler waves of alpha. Fresh creative energy begins to flow, emotions stabilize, and a person experiences a liberating sense of peace and well-being. The alpha state is where meditation starts, and the brain can begin to access the wealth of creativity that lies just below conscious awareness.

- **Theta waves:** As the brain goes deeper into relaxation, the brain enters the theta state, where brain activity slows almost to the point of sleep. The theta state enables heightened receptivity, flashes of dreamlike imagery, and inspiration and sometimes can bring long-forgotten memories to light.

- **Delta waves:** The delta state is the slowest type of brain-wave activity, and occurs during deep, dreamless sleep.

Positively accessing both alpha and theta waves has been shown to have an effect on concentration, creativity, and stress levels. Through exercise, breathing, and meditation techniques—some of which are detailed in Essential 4: Mindfulness, Essential 5: Memory, and Essential 6: Emotional Wellness—Brain Power helps students establish a healthy brain wave balance throughout the day.

CHAPTER 3

The Five Steps to a Power Brain

I am not what happened to me; I am what I choose to become.
– Carl Jung

The Brain Education method works in five steps that move from brain awakening all the way to brain mastery. The Brain Power program follows this systematic approach to help students grow into their true potential. The steps are a linked series of exercises that are practical, easy, and fun and are organized to coincide with the structure and functions of the brain as well as its physiological characteristics.

STEP 1: BRAIN SENSITIZING

- **Purpose:** Awakens the brain-body senses through physical activity.
- **Benefits:** Stimulates circulation of blood, oxygen, and energy to the brain while enhancing awareness of the brain and its functions.
- **Classroom Application:** One-minute easy and fun

physical exercises boost focus and increase attention span.

In this step, students become acutely aware of the brain and its functions while strengthening the connection between the body and the brain. Stretching exercises emphasizing the mind-body interaction are used to establish Brain Sensitizing. As each muscle in the body is moved and every nerve is stimulated, the corresponding areas of the brain are awakened. As a result, balance and coordination improve in the body. Simple and engaging meditation techniques are used to help students release stress that may be hindering their academic performance, while helping them develop greater mental clarity and focus. Confidence in their abilities is fostered as well through activities that challenge them and their preconceptions of their capabilities.

Activity example: 3-6-0 (p. 106); Push-ups (p. 102).

STEP 2: BRAIN VERSATILIZING

- **Purpose:** Creates new neural circuitry while connecting the different parts of the brain.
- **Benefits:** Introduces mental flexibility that frees students from fixed habits, opens the brain to new information, and makes it more adaptable and resilient.
- **Classroom Application:** Challenging neuroplasticity exercises to improve mental coordination and teach mental endurance and positive resilience.

The limits of our happiness and success are often dictated by preconceptions and prior experiences, especially those that have hardened into habits. Brain Versatilizing rewires even the strongest neural connections underlying preconceptions and habits by helping students make new associations, stimulating their creativity, and introducing positive thought patterns. These new connections are reinforced by success in the Brain Power activities and positive affirmations from self, peers, and teachers. Even deeply embedded prejudices and preconceptions such as "I'm not good at math," "I've never been popular," and "Things never work out for me," can be changed.

In the process of actively and consciously making new neural circuits, the brain becomes very adaptable and students become able to learn more easily and quickly. They face new situations and challenges more readily. Brain Versatilizing catalyzes new healthy habits, which can turn a student's life around.

Activity example: Pinky-Thumb (p. 113); Harmony Claps (p. 115).

STEP 3. BRAIN REFRESHING

- **Purpose:** Releases negative emotional memories and habits.
- **Benefits:** Invites a more positive, hopeful, and empowering mindset.
- **Classroom Application:** Simple and effective mindfulness and emotional release exercises promote happiness and harmony among students. Training to release negative emotional memories and habits clears away emotional residues of early traumatic experiences and redirects the associated energy toward new perspectives and attitudes.

In some ways, this step is akin to rebooting a computer. Throughout a student's life, he or she has accumulated experiences that were written into the operating system of his or her brain. All later experiences were processed and interpreted by this operating system, leaving students unconsciously controlled by them. The most robust programs written were those created by experiences charged with strong emotions. When negative, these dysfunctional programs prevent students from reaching their full potential, just as when my students tore up their baseline assessments and said, "Why take it, if we are going to fail anyway?"

Brain Refreshing provides students with the means to rewrite their own brain operating system. Brain Power exercises remove the residue of past emotions, making it easier to change the programs associated with them. They also teach students awareness of their emotions, both past and present, and offer clear and simple strategies for changing them. The mindfulness students then acquire through experience allows them to choose their emotions and thoughts and write their own brain code as they go through their lives.

Activity example: Energy Ball Visualization (p. 122); HSP Breathing (p. 149).

STEP 4: BRAIN INTEGRATING

- **Purpose:** Integrates the different functional areas of the brain—the brain stem, limbic system, and neocortex—and improves communication and cooperative interaction between the brain's right and left hemispheres.
- **Benefits:** Brain Integration helps a student revisit core information affecting his or her life and awakens the brain stem to coordinate physical, emotional, and cognitive power.
- **Classroom Application:** Integrative exercises such as endurance training, visualization, and mindfulness help

students feel powerful, focused, and confident.

After clearing the charge of past emotions, students become ready to integrate new thought patterns and behaviors. By engaging both sides of their brain and all three layers—physical, emotional, and cognitive—the new patterns are fully embedded into their brain. Students take on a new identity, one that believes in their abilities and dreams of an exciting future. The self-efficacy they develop aids their academic performance and the formation of meaningful relationships. It also motivates them to set and achieve goals, both by themselves and with a team.

Brain Integrating also involves greater awareness of the interconnectedness between self, other people, and the planet. Students observe the ripple effects of their actions with honesty and sincerity, and adjust their behavior to the needs of the group or greater good.

Activity example: HSP Gym (p. 159); Brain Declaration (p. 186).

STEP 5: BRAIN MASTERING

- **Purpose:** Helps achieve greater executive control over the brain.
- **Benefits:** Helps students make proactive decisions and positive choices.
- **Classroom Application:** Consistent practice in relevant goal-setting and leadership activities helps students gain self-trust and feel their personal value.

Brain Mastering is the process of designing the life you want by clearly defining your goals based on your values and practicing

Steps 1 through 4 to achieve them. This ongoing process turns a brain into a Power Brain that energizes one's life.

Brain mastery means exercising choice. Knowing they have a choice and being empowered to enact their choices turns students into leaders with good character and integrity who can find creative solutions to life's challenges.

Activity example: I Have a Dream (p. 178); Altruistic Actions (p. 191).

As you progress through the exercises of the ten Essentials in Part 2 of this book, you and your students will naturally move through these five steps. Just as each exercise incorporates multiple layers of the brain and areas of life, they also help students practice more than one step. For example, even simple push-ups strengthen the body and circulate more blood, relieve emotions, and inspire "I can do it" confidence. Perfecting any one of the steps is a lifelong journey, and the skills in earlier steps will continue to be used in later ones.

STEP 5: Brain Mastering

- Empowers authorship of life purpose.
- Enables greater executive control of the brain.
- Expedites decision-making process.

STEP 4: Brain Integrating

- Unites diverse areas of the brain.
- Enhances communication between hemispheres.
- Releases latent abilities.

STEP 3: Brain Refreshing

- Clears away emotional residue.
- Encourages positive life view.
- Develops emotional intelligence.

STEP 2: Brain Versatilizing

- Creates flexibility in brain circuitry.
- Frees brain from rigid habits.
- Opens practitioner to new information.

STEP 1: Brain Sensitizing

- Awakens the five senses.
- Improves physiological functioning.
- Encourages brain awareness.

FIVE STEPS OF BRAIN EDUCATION

CHAPTER 4

The Multiple Intelligences of a Power Brain

We should spend less time ranking children and more time helping them to identify their natural competencies and gifts and cultivate these.
– Howard Gardner

In his 1983 book, *Frames of Mind*, Harvard psychologist Howard Gardner famously suggested a theory of eight multiple intelligences, which are useful in guiding any holistic approach to education, including Brain Education. We all learn in different ways, and research shows that teaching methods that engage a variety of learning styles not only help students by engaging their dominant mode of learning, they also help students develop other forms of intelligence, which builds a stronger, more integrated brain. Through teaching to multiple intelligences, students literally become more intelligent in every sense of the word.

Instead of a one-size-fits-all idea of intelligence, Gardner's theory divides human capability into the following: visual-spatial intelligence, linguistic-verbal intelligence, logical-mathematical intelligence, bodily-kinesthetic intelligence, musical intelligence, interpersonal intelligence, intrapersonal intelligence, and naturalistic intelligence.

So, what does Multiple Intelligence theory have to do with the Brain Power Classroom? Many, including Gardner himself, argue that our traditional school system, including the majority of assessments that seek to measure student achievement, focuses almost exclusively on logical-mathematical and linguistic forms of intelligence. Brain Power provides hundreds of activities, thirty of which are included in this book, that tap into all eight of Gardner's intelligences.

Additionally, according to Thomas Armstrong, author of the outstanding book, *Multiple Intelligences in the Classroom*, "Intelligences usually work together in complex ways." Brain Power activities such as Harmony Claps (p. 115), Pinky-Thumb (p. 113), and 3-6-0 Belly Drumming (p. 106) tap into five or more forms of intelligence simultaneously, making for an exciting and enriching mental workout for students. By employing Brain Power, teachers are able to build engaging tasks into lessons that allow students to interact with content in ways that fit their unique learning styles and strengths.

- **Visual-Spatial Intelligence:** Drawing infinity signs (p. 128) engages visual abilities while calming brain waves and making connections between the left and right hemispheres. Visualization exercises such as imagining negative emotions being released from the brain (p. 149) or picturing your goals being achieved on a BrainScreen (p. 134) also build up students' visual ability. Partner stretching exercises (p. 93) build gross and fine motor skills and help students become more aware of their spatial environment.

- **Linguistic-Verbal Intelligence:** Brain Power exercises teach students how to use empowering words to describe themselves and their fellow students. They give

MULTIPLE INTELLIGENCES

each other compliments (p. 176), learn the power of positive self-talk, share their experiences with each other, and declare positive attributes and goals, such as the Brain Declaration (p. 186).

- **Logical-Mathematical Intelligence:** By increasing oxygen flow to the brain and making complex or abstract ideas familiar and based in experience, Brain Power amplifies logical-mathematical intelligence. Students engage in problem solving activities such as Balloon Challenge (p. 95) and Pinky-Thumb (p. 113), which build their logical intelligence. Additionally, many Brain Power games involve creative counting and reinforce number facts and math skills. Students also learn to "Persist through Positivity" (p. 80), which builds the emotional resilience necessary to use logical-mathematical intelligence to solve challenging academic prompts.

- **Bodily-Kinesthetic Intelligence:** Most Brain Power exercises involve a physical element and not only improve dexterity and balance and enhance the mind-body connection, but also reinforce academic content through physical exercise. For example, Harmony Claps (p. 115) can be effectively used to teach kinesthetic learners their multiplication facts, while Bullfrog Belly (p. 136) and other core exercises that illustrate the "Water Up, Fire Down" health principle (p. 108) can be used to help students understand the scientific concept of photosynthesis.

- **Musical Intelligence:** Brain Power incorporates music into its program, using singing, dancing, and exercises to music and/or rhythm to aid performance and change thoughts, emotions, and atmosphere. Students learn to express themselves through singing, drawing to music (Listen and Draw, p. 165), moving to rhythm (Create-a-Dance, p. 169), and expressing positive affirmations (Self Declaration, p. 157). Brain Power Wellness also trains teachers how to facilitate student assemblies that showcase a variety of artistic representations of what students have learned from the program.

- **Interpersonal Intelligence:** Brain Power provides effective means for students to interact with each other in a positive way. Through engaging team building activities such as partner stretching (Sky-Earth-Friend, p. 93) and the Wow Wow rhythm clapping exercise (p. 117), students learn about the importance of nonverbal communication—body language, eye contact, facial gestures, etc. The Compliment Game (p. 176) helps students learn positive communication and become comfortable with expressing their emotions. In addition, students learn to use exercises such as push-ups to release strong emotions before engaging with others. Through character education, such as the Altruistic Actions activity (p. 191), students learn how to communicate and connect sincerely with others.

- **Intrapersonal Intelligence:** Brain Power encourages mindfulness and meditation, giving students space and time to really get to know themselves. Students learn meditations such as feeling an energy ball (p. 122), breathing techniques (HSP Breathing, p. 149), and Infinity Drawing (p. 128), all of which give students tools to look inward. Confident Qualities (p. 154) encourages students to reflect on their inner strength, while activities such as I Have a Dream (p. 178) help students search inside to find their authentic life goals.

- **Naturalistic Intelligence:** Brain Power not only emphasizes a deeper and more meaningful connection to oneself and other people, it builds a stronger connection to the earth itself. Students learn the Earth Kid Concept, which introduces humanity's dependency on the earth and its role in taking care of it. Through activities such as Earth Challenges & Solutions (p. 189), students reflect on their appreciation for the earth and grow their leadership as "Earth Citizens" who want to help create a healthier, more sustainable future.

Emotional Intelligence

Another kind of intelligence, called Emotional Intelligence, has been championed by many, including Daniel Goleman and researchers John D. Mayer and Peter Salovey. Emotional Intelligence refers to the ability to perceive, control, and evaluate emotions, both within oneself and in other people. It involves determining which emotions are present in oneself or someone else, using emotions to guide what one pays attention to and how one evaluates a situation, understanding the meaning or cause behind an emotion, responding appropriately to emotions, and managing them. In the context of multiple intelligences, Emotional Intelligence plays a role in both interpersonal and intrapersonal intelligence. Activities such as Emotional Inventory (p. 146), Laughing Exercise (p. 148), and HSP Smile Breathing (p. 149) help students develop Emotional Intelligence.

CHAPTER 5

The Oxygen Mask Principle

You can't give what you don't have.
– Unknown

Fifty years ago, teacher and child psychologist Haim Ginott said:

> *I've come to the frightening conclusion that I am the decisive element in the classroom. It's my personal approach that creates the climate. It's my daily mood that makes the weather. As a teacher, I possess a tremendous power to make a child's life miserable or joyous. I can be a tool of torture or an instrument of inspiration. I can humiliate or heal. In all situations, it is my response that decides whether a crisis will be escalated or de-escalated and a child humanized or dehumanized.*

His words are truer now than ever. Think of a recent interaction with a student that you now regret. You may have raised your voice, dismissed them, embarrassed them, or ignored their concern. Now, reflect on your feeling prior to and during that encounter. How was your energy level? Your stress level? What was your emotional state in that moment? Chances are, your energy was low and your stress levels were high. It's very simple: When teachers are physically healthy, energized, happy, passionate, creative, focused, and confident, they are simply better at what they do. When we feel good, we do good. The research-based brain exercises and activities that comprise Brain Power have been proven not only to improve student health and achievement, they engage and tend to teachers' multiple needs!

Working with children in any capacity is a rewarding and life-affirming calling; however, it can also be tremendously stressful. Without a system of proactive tools for adults to have on hand, it is more difficult to manage the unpredictability each day brings. Then a vicious cycle ensues, as if a teacher were on an airplane that was slowly losing cabin pressure and oxygen. The harder it becomes to breathe, the more stressed the person; the more stressed, the harder it is to breathe. During the safety demonstrations every airline is mandated to give passengers, the flight attendants explain that in the unlikely event the cabin loses pressure, adults should "put their masks on first before assisting others." This principle has become popularly known as the Oxygen Mask Principle, which aims to explain that it is not selfish to tend to oneself before the needs of others—it is wise. What does this mean for educators?

When the following likely events occur, they could be losing oxygen:

- Physical exhaustion or low energy
- Brain fog or sluggishness
- Physical ailments, including headaches, digestive problems, joint pain, insomnia, etc.
- Difficulty managing emotions and staying positive
- Loss of concentration or memory
- Feelings of being "stuck," and/or loss of motivation or autonomy

- Combative social or professional relationships

If any of these are the case for you, please take oxygen now. Oxygen is abundant throughout Part 2 of this book, within the very exercises teachers will offer their own students for the same purposes of tending to emotional, physical, and mental wellness.

This principle is also critical because it reminds educators that how they sometimes feel is really no different than how students feel. The fact that we are all human, some just older than others, raises teacher empathy and compassion for students' own classroom and learning challenges. This further enables educators to help students help themselves to manage their own wellness with Brain Power tools designed to last a lifetime. When there is solidarity between students and teachers, research shows a tremendous impact on student performance.

Manage Stress!

Is stress good or bad? Both. Moderate stress helps keep us alert, attentive, and efficient. However, when stress goes unmitigated, it can lead to physical and mental challenges. In fact, anxiety is the number one reason students underperform on school assessments. Additionally, research shows that prolonged stress actually shrinks brain cells in the hippocampus, the region of the brain responsible for memory.

Brain Power's mindful breathing, visualization exercises, and physical activity help activate the parasympathetic nervous system, which controls rest and digestion, to balance the levels of stress hormones in the body and brain. When you want to help control your or your students' stress and anxiety, try one of the Mindfulness activities (Essential 4) in Part 2.

CHAPTER 6

Classroom Management: From Control to Collaboration

Alone we can do so little; together we can do so much.
– Helen Keller

If one of the most important indicators of student performance is the relationship between a student and teacher, how can we ensure a positive one? Educators need to have control over their classroom, but often it is the misunderstanding of what control means that disrupts the balance of the classroom. It is a paradox I discovered in my own classroom, as I mentioned in the Introduction. When control is misused, it turns into an insidious enemy of progress, which I call the control paradigm. The most obvious limitation is that such an approach solicits one of two student responses: compliance or defiance.

Defiance or Compliance? Which one would you like to have from your students? Any teacher who has sought to complete a learning objective for thirty students can tell you defiance is not a desirable student attribute. Defiance in all its forms—confrontation, refusal to cooperate, resistance, disobedience—poses a clear roadblock to creating a productive and engaging learning environment. Therefore, it is usually compliance that seems like a better option. But is it really?

For a moment, brainstorm three to five attribute goals you have for your students or your own child. How was it? Chances are you came up with things like "independent thinker," "compassionate leader," "creative problem solver," etc. Most of us want our students and our own children to grow as independent and critical thinkers and creative leaders. I'm willing to bet the words "submissive" or "docile" didn't make your mental list. But this is precisely what we promote when we praise compliance. Perhaps this is why famous creative thinkers like Oprah Winfrey, Steve Jobs, Maya Angelou, Ilchi Lee, and even Albert Einstein didn't fit into the traditional school model.

In his book, *Power vs. Force,* David Hawkins details the difference between force and power. Force, he says, is exhibited through lower-level consciousness emotions such as anger and judgment, while power is rooted in higher-level consciousness emotions like acceptance and joy.

Our job as educators, therefore, is not to *force* students into compliance; it is to use our inner *power* to inspire students to put forth their best effort. The system of force and the need to control are rooted in fear. Power and the collaboration that results are rooted in love.

In working with thousands of educators around the world, I have found teachers to be some of the most warm-hearted, compassionate, and dedicated people on the planet. I would argue that almost all teachers were drawn to teaching because they love children and want to help create a brighter future. The twenty-five tips that follow, and all the information in this book, are designed to help educators create systems in their classrooms that reflect this love by moving from the paradigm of control to harmonious collaboration.

CONTROL	COLLABORATION
Students should respect teachers	Everyone should respect everyone
Students have two choices: compliance or defiance	Students participate with active engagement
Teacher's role is to be the "Sage on the Stage"	Teacher's role is to be the "Guide on the Side"
Students must listen to the teacher and peers with respect and speak respectfully and effectively	Students listen to their teacher and peers with empathy; they develop intrapersonal awareness to communicate harmoniously
The teacher creates the task and mode of assessment	The students choose and/or create the task and modes of assessment
Teacher-student relationship: hierarchy and struggle	Teacher-student dynamic: equality and harmony
Education = Teach students academic skills	Education = Draw out students' inner greatness to help them maximize their life potential
Motivation = Extrinsic	Motivation = Intrinsic

COMPARISON OF CONTROL VS. COLLABORATION

A NOTE ABOUT DISCIPLINE

The collaborative classroom does not mean eliminating discipline. Indeed, effective discipline is designed to invite positive behavior and proactively avoid negative behavior. Discipline should be about accountability and growth, not punishment. The tone educators set in a classroom has a huge impact on student behavior. When educators have positive expectations and focus their attention on positive results, students are more likely to behave in a manner that begets success.

Brain Power Classroom Rules

The Latin root of educate means "to draw out." What are we drawing out of our students? Their infinite potential, their creativity, their natural beauty, and genius. Therefore, if we are drawing these abilities out, it means they already exist. Our job, as educators, is to help our students remove the limiting factors that are concealing this potential. Remind students to, above all things . . .

- Do Your Best
- Be Confident
- Be Positive
- Be Honest and Responsible
- Trust Your Brain

CHAPTER 7

Tips for a Brain Power Classroom

If you want small changes in your life, work on your attitude. But if you want big and primary changes, work on your paradigm.
– Stephen Covey

Creating a collaborative classroom that waters and fertilizes Power Brains can be as simple as adjusting your mindset and incorporating a few new but tested behaviors. Involving students in class decisions, being mindful of and actively using nonverbal communication, and creating a positive environment in which teacher and students compliment and promote positive behaviors can make dramatic improvements in students' self-efficacy and success. This approach addresses the parts of the child that textbooks cannot and models the emotional regulation and social behaviors that students need to learn.

The following twenty-five tips, which are based on research and classroom experience, prescribe the changes that can turn your classroom into a Brain Power Classroom in detail. Use the ones you think will work for your class, and let them inspire you to innovate and create your own.

Get Students Involved

1. Rule Together

Invite students to help you establish class rules that will help each member of the learning community flourish (e.g., see Brain Power Rules on p. 66). Facilitate unanimous agreement on the rules. When there is a breakdown, remind the students about the rule and express your confidence in them to make the proper adjustments. Instead of lecturing, sincerely ask them, "Are you following rule number three right now?" Remind them of the purpose of the rule: to help them maximize their potential.

2. Teach Democracy over Dictatorship

In addition to involving your students in making the rules, give them a voice in day-to-day operations to help them take ownership of the learning process. Taking a class vote regarding the order of subjects taught, the destination of a field trip, or how the class can celebrate an upcoming holiday, teaches students about the democratic process and encourages participation. Providing options on such things as subject matter of project topics, modes of assessment (essay, video, documentary, illustration), and individual versus group work, helps students take ownership of their learning.

3. Facilitate Class Jobs

Creating class jobs is a wonderful way to help students take responsibility for their classroom while learning teamwork and time management. While you can certainly suggest certain jobs, asking students themselves to brainstorm jobs they feel will help the classroom atmosphere invokes immediate ownership for them. Allow the class to vote on the jobs created, how to fairly rotate, how to ensure quality control, etc.

Cultivate Leaders

4. Take Me to Your Leader

Many times, students who tend to exhibit challenging behaviors also possess innate leadership skills. In Part 2 of this book, you will read about Jeffrey, who was often in trouble for not using his leadership potential for good. However, working with him created a positive ripple effect that reached the students who liked to follow Jeffrey. Finding the natural leaders in your classroom and getting them on board with spreading the culture you want to instill is a must. Win the respect and trust of these leaders, and allow them to help you create an atmosphere of harmonious collaboration.

5. Encourage Energy Masters and Peer Teaching

Research shows that peer teaching results in significant cognitive gains for both the "teacher" and student. Once you have taught some basic Brain Power exercises and routines to your class, you will be able to encourage peer teaching of Brain Power. Each day, choose two Energy Masters (preferably one boy and one girl) to lead Brain Power exercises. Earning this honor could be a reward for the previous day's performance, improvement in homework, class participation, good citizenship, etc. Once students have demonstrated positive leadership in teaching Brain Power within your class, team up with another teacher and give students the opportunity to lead activities for other classes as well.

Use Positive Praise

6. Start from the Start

Each morning, greet students happily and genuinely at the door. We are here to teach students, not curriculum, so take a moment to share a smile, high-five, or hug as each student walks in to establish a nurturing, positive tone for the day. Check in with students who are prone to disruptive behavior; connect with them on a personal level first and help them choose to create a great day.

7. Give Three-to-One Praise

Catch students "being good" three times more often than you criticize negative behavior or performance. One principle of Brain Education is, "Where your mind goes, energy follows." In other words, we get more of what we focus on. By consistently pointing out what students do right, you can guide them to grow those qualities and behaviors and develop positive attitudes. All of us need and want attention, and one way or another, we will get it. If a student sees that you react to his negative behavior, you are enforcing that behavior and ensuring it will continue.

No matter how constructive the feedback, if we fail to recognize our students' attributes, we run the risk of undermining their confidence. The Three-to-One Principle helps create a safe, nurturing environment that celebrates positive effort and minimizes negativity.

An important note about praise: Compliments are great, but not all praise is created equal. Instead of offering general praise, try modeling specific, character-based praise that celebrates effort and attitude. For example, instead of, "Your hair looks pretty today!" try, "Ella, your homework reflects real effort. I can tell you did your best. Great job!"

While it is certainly acceptable to help students feel good

about their physical appearance, praise shouldn't stop there. In addition to encouraging positive behavior and attitudes, the purpose of praise should be to cultivate intrinsic motivation within students. According to Carol Dweck's influential book, *Mindset*, when we say things like, "You are so smart!" or "You are so good at basketball!" we may actually be doing harm. Why? Because we condition students to rely on motivation from our general praise *of them* rather than enhancing an internal drive to succeed that reflects their *inner* morality. Comments like, "I see you did well on your math test; it looks like your hard work paid off," help students feel proud of their choice to study hard, thereby enforcing that behavior. Rather than telling students how they should feel, comments like this invite self-reflection that internalizes the feeling of pride and self-respect. Effective praise is akin to the Chinese proverb, "Give a man a fish and you feed him for a day. Teach him how to fish and you feed him for a lifetime."

Type	Compliment	Feeling	Outcome
Extrinsic	"You are so smart!"	I like it when my teacher says I'm smart.	I want to keep doing things to get my teacher to think I'm smart.
Intrinsic	"I see you did well on your math test. Congratulations! It looks like your hard work paid off. How does that feel?"	When I work hard I get results and feel proud of myself.	I am motivated to keep working hard so I can perform my best.

COMPARISON OF COMPLIMENT STYLES

8. Play the Compliment Game

Just as we want to start the day positively, ending the day on a high note completes the tone of a Brain Power Classroom. At the end of the day, create a habit of complimenting students on projects, participation, good behavior, kind gestures, etc. (see Compliment Game on p. 176). Invite students to praise one another and then themselves. This approach to compliments demonstrates that harmony in the classroom relies not only on the student-teacher dynamic but also on how students relate to themselves personally and to each other, thus enhancing all three of the primary classroom relationships (see diagram on p. 34).

9. Pull for Their Inner Greatness

When students present challenging behaviors, it can feel like a battle of "us versus them." Resist the temptation to be "right" or "teach them a lesson." Instead of speaking to the behavior, try to go deeper to the underlying issue. Negative behavior almost always attributes to poor self-esteem. Habits are formed over time, but they are not fixed. Indeed, positive behavior can be learned, practiced, and cultivated. Every student has a pure spirit—help them grow it! When we speak to our students' inner greatness, we help them grow into the highest versions of themselves.

10. Do Ask, Don't Tell

If in doubt, ask a question. When we ask intelligent questions of our students, rather than giving them "the answer" we want through a statement, we invite critical thinking and encourage inquisitiveness. Try to ask focused but open-ended questions. Instead of "Doesn't that character remind you of last week's protagonist?" ask, "Does this character remind you of another protagonist we've studied recently? In what way?" This habit of intelligent questioning applies to helping students make academic connections, as well as encouraging intrapersonal awareness through reflecting on social situations. Instead of saying, "That wasn't a nice thing to say to her," ask, "How could you have handled that differently?" Instead of stating, "Bryan, I know you can do better than this," ask, "Bryan, does this work reflect your best effort?" Just as specific and meaningful praise motivates students intrinsically, encouraging them to evaluate themselves and the world around them critically through intelligent questions helps students take ownership of their academic and social learning.

Go Beyond Words

11. Use Proximity and Space

A social psychologist at Harvard University, Amy Cuddy, in her captivating TED Talk about the power of body language, explains that our brains are wired to hear nonverbal messages and cues over verbal ones. Moving our bodies closer toward students, making eye contact, putting a hand on one's shoulder, or even inflecting the voice are all ways of using proximity and space, which is more effective than yelling across the room. As Cuddy explains, the messages we send with our bodies are delivered at a much higher volume than what comes out of our mouths. When a student loses focus, is off task, or disruptive, don't break your focus by explicitly pointing out the student's negative behavior ("Kevin, are you with us? Can you pay attention please?"). This is a sure-fire way to embarrass the student (which invites resentment and revenge), and shows the rest of the class that the best way to get your attention is to misbehave. This approach takes your attention off the lesson and models distractedness while compromising the class's learning efficiency.

Instead, use what Doug Lemov, author of *Teach Like a Champion 2.0*, calls "nonverbal intervention": take two steps toward the child who needs refocusing, make knowing eye contact with the daydreamer, or raise the pitch of your voice enthusiastically to reenergize the class.

12. Excite with Body Language

Body language also works to keep students engaged. Move around the room as you address the class. Use your facial expressions, hand gestures, and posture to connect with students.

Also, encourage students to sit and stand up straight and demonstrate confident body language for their own purposes. This engages our body's energy center and straightens our spine, therefore improving blood, oxygen, and energy flow to the brain.

As researched by social psychologist Amy Cuddy, "power posing" helps build confidence and even lowers stress hormone levels. "Our bodies change our minds and our minds can change behavior," she explains, "and our behavior can change our outcomes."

You don't have to pretend to be a superhero to reap the benefits. Simply sitting up straight or uncrossing your legs and planting your feet firmly on the ground can raise attention levels. Periodically practicing stretching and core strengthening exercises will make it easier for students to sit up straight, while mindfulness training (see Essential 4, p. 119) connects them to their bodies, so they can maintain good posture.

13. Make Eye Contact on Their Level

When you need to speak with a student about a personal issue, including inappropriate behavior, make sure to lower your posture physically so that you are on "their level." Sit or kneel down across from them, make eye contact, and communicate clearly. Try this simple role-play with a colleague:

- A partner (the student) sits in a chair while you (the teacher) stand. Talk briefly with the student about a problem, for instance, tardiness.
- Repeat the same scenario, this time kneeling or sitting down across the student.
- Switch roles, and repeat the exercise.
- Discussion: How did it feel when the teacher was standing over you versus sitting across from you? Did you notice any other changes occur in the seated position, as in body language or in tone or volume of voice? Did the content of what the teacher said change in relation to standing and sitting? Did the response from the student change based on the teacher's position?

14. Tone, Pace, and Volume

Again, because our brains are wired to pick up nonverbal cues over verbal ones, the way in which we speak goes a lot further in communicating our true feelings and attitudes. The adage, "It's not what you say; it's how you say it" is at play here. Be aware of the energy you project through your voice. Consistently talking loudly, quickly, or repeating yourself actually trains students to block you out. Always be aware of your tone of voice and the emotional response it elicits from your students. When in doubt, try to talk succinctly in a quiet volume and gentle tone—you may be surprised to see your students listening more intently.

15. Use Power Brain Clapping

We all lose focus; it's inevitable. Power Brain Clapping is a useful class management tool that grabs students' attention and helps them focus on the speaker.

1) Clap the hands five times in a distinct rhythm: slow, slow, fast, fast, fast.

2) Invite students to join you in repeating the rhythm: slow, slow, fast, fast, fast.

3) After clapping, students raise their hands up as they say, "Power!" and pull their fists strongly down as they say, "Brain!"

4) After Power Brain Clapping, students' eyes should be on the teacher, ears open, mouths closed (but smiling), sitting straight.

5) Once the class learns the clapping sequence, it can be used in the future as a signal that you need the students' attention. This mitigates the "us versus them" mentality and turns the classroom into a scream-free, harmonious, and collaborative environment. If you'd like to instill a more democratic practice, invite the students to create a rhythm they prefer and designate it as your classroom's Power Brain Clap.

16. I Repeat: Do Not Repeat Yourself

We all want to be heard. We also want to help our students improve their listening skills. For many of us, it can be tempting, when addressing the whole class, to repeat what you say several times (often at higher and higher volumes) to make sure every student "gets it." In addition, some teachers continue calling a given student's name over and over again when trying to get their attention. These techniques, rather than helping build listening skills, actually train our students to not listen to us the first time. ("I mean, why bother listening the first time if she is just going to repeat herself two or three more times?") When we need to deliver information to the entire class, make sure you have everyone's attention (Power Brain Clapping is an excellent technique for this) and speak concisely, at a sensible volume.

Allow Time to Refresh

17. Take Brain Breaks

Research shows that the average adult brain needs to take breaks at least every ninety minutes and the brains of students need to be refreshed even more often. It may initially seem like a waste of time, but breaking often, even in the middle of what seems like a productive lesson, will lead to more focus and long-term memory in the long run. Brain Education recommends students be given at least one "brain break" per lesson. This helps create a fun, active, and challenging atmosphere. Every activity in this book can be used as a brain break. See "Brain Power Activities for Your Classroom" on page 82 for brain breaks that are "Energizers," "Mood Changers," or "Calming and Centering" to help you optimize your students' energy levels throughout the day.

18. Physical Exercise for Emotional Release

When students are frustrated, angry, or emotional, instead of lecturing or "talking at students" (who aren't in the proper frame of mind to listen, no matter how well-meaning your words may be) first give them the space to literally shake it off. Taking a walk or getting a drink of water can be enough for some upset children, however, adding specific Brain Power exercises teaches them tools for self-regulation that can last a lifetime. To help students regulate and improve their moods, encourage them to try some of the activities in Essential 2: Physical Health and Essential 6: Emotional Wellness in Part 2 of this book.

19. Create a Brain Power Station

Having a designated "safe" space in the classroom where students know they can find sanctuary helps reinforce a Brain Power Classroom. Instead of disrupting a lesson, teach students to self-regulate by independently visiting the station to use a specific Brain Power activity for whatever need they have. Tired? No problem! Frustrated? We got you! Feeling hyperactive? No sweat! Many teachers post Brain Power posters, print outs of the Brain Declaration (see p. 186), brain games, or step-by-step illustrations of Brain Education exercises. After a few minutes, students will have proactively and productively refreshed their emotional, mental, or physical energy—all on their own.

Create Calm and Connection

20. De-escalate Conflict

It is easy to add fuel to the fire of conflict by mixing in your own emotions. When students have an interpersonal dispute, model how to manage emotions, instead of joining in. When you are upset, take your oxygen first, breathing in a few deep breaths before speaking. Use Brain Power exercises to change your energy first, so you can help students address their own situations with cool heads.

21. Teach Empathetic Listening, Intrapersonal Awareness, and Problem Solving

As described in Arthur Costa and Bena Kallick's book, *Habits of Mind*, listening with understanding and empathy is one of the hallmarks of a harmonious and productive classroom. As teachers, we know that it is important for students to have good listening skills, but not simply for the sake of docility. Students who listen to their teacher and peers with empathy can't do so without also listening to their own inner voices, and this introspection is key to growth and learning. Whenever possible, ask students to reflect on how they think their actions (negative or positive) made their peers feel. Also, ask them how they felt when they behaved a certain way. Help them find and trust their inner sense of morality. Asking students these questions invites them to see the situation differently and take ownership of how they decide to solve conflicts.

- **Empathy** → "How do you think she felt when you said that?"
- **Intrapersonal Awareness** → "How did it feel in your heart when you said that?"
- **Problem Solving** → "What can we do to make it right?"

22. Remember They Feel What You Feel
We are all human and respond in similar ways to outside influences. If you see the class squirming, losing focus, or daydreaming, think about how you feel. Are you becoming fatigued? Most likely, your students are, too. Are they frustrated or tense? Use empathy and self-awareness to "read the room" and keep the energy positive and collaborative. If things don't feel right, then it's the perfect time for a brain break to change the mood. You're all in this together!

23. Model, Model, Model
As we know, "Do as I say, not as I do," and other remnants of the control paradigm simply don't work in the long run. Use your power, harnessing the good you have inside yourself, to bring out the best in your students. Modeling good behavior is similar to the body language effect we now know to be impactful.

If you can stay composed, speak calmly, use breathing exercises, or solve conflicts peacefully, most likely students will turn to your techniques when they need them most. Dictating to students how they should solve problems or how to act when angry doesn't turn them into independent problem solvers or critical thinkers. Modeling helps students make observable strategies their own, return to them autonomously, and form intrinsic motivations that inspire growth.

Build Their Strength

24. Inspire Competitive Cooperation

From the perspective of building character, the competition's ostensible result—"winning" or "losing"—is ultimately secondary. Students will learn soon enough that they can't win them all, but Brain Power aims to teach that our choice to give sincere effort, despite the outcome, is always within our control.

- Did you do your best?
- Did you have fun?
- Did you support your team?

These are the most meaningful questions to ask students following any competition.

Using the exercises in Essential 1: Team Building in Part 2 of this book and asking students to reflect on the above questions regardless of the task's result will help them learn the true value of competition.

25. Persist Through Positivity

When we introduce challenging Brain Power exercises—or any

new concept—it is normal for students to experience some level of frustration or resistance. The primary difference between students who succeed and fail at a given task is the propensity to quit or persevere. Brain Power offers these three tips to help students persist through positivity.

- **Smile.** When we smile, our brain releases endorphins that not only make us feel happier, but actually improve our cognitive functioning. Smiling lowers stress levels and reduces anxiety while creating the positive brain chemistry that improves information processing and creativity.

- **Breathe Out.** There are more than 100,000 miles of blood vessels in our brain. When we become tense, our breathing becomes shallow, which inhibits blood flow and prevents oxygen and vital nutrients from entering our brain. When we breathe out, we activate the parasympathetic nervous system, which facilitates the "rest and digest" mode and promotes healthy blood and oxygen flow to our brain. This relaxed and rejuvenated state makes it easier to maintain a positive mood and attitude.

- **Say, "I Can Do It."** Over the last several years, the field of positive psychology has unequivocally proven a direct link between a student's self-efficacy, or belief in their ability, and their success at a given task. When we are under stress, it is normal for our internal monologue to turn negative. Encourage your students to engage in positive self-talk, either silently or aloud, including: "I can do it!" "I'm a Power Brain!" "I got this!" and "My brain loves challenges!" This self-talk will help them release tension and persevere with a positive mindset.

Brain Power Activities for Your Classroom

In Part 2, you will be introduced to the ten Essentials of a Brain Power Classroom. As you learn more about the principles and techniques of the thirty activities that follow, I hope you will start to see how incorporating these simple, short, and engaging "brain breaks" into your day can be individualized to your particular classroom needs.

What is important is that you begin to create the Brain Power habit, wherein you are consistently using Brain Power activities to create the optimal classroom atmosphere. Eventually, this will lead your students to begin to self-regulate by independently using Brain Power exercises as they need them. As discussed in Tip 20, creating a Brain Power Station (with posters, space for exercise, workbooks, printouts, art supplies, etc.) in your room is highly recommended. Below is a sample of how Brain Power exercises can be used throughout the day and to tend to many different challenges and needs.

Morning Routine
- 3-6-0 Belly Drumming (p. 106)
- Bullfrog Belly (p. 136)
- Sky-Earth-Friend (p. 93)
- BrainScreen (p. 134)

Transitions
- Power Brain Clapping (p. 75)
- Pinky-Thumb (p. 113)
- Harmony Clap (p. 115)

Before a Test
- Wow Wow (p. 117)
- Energy Ball (p. 122)
- 3-6-0 Belly Drumming (p. 106)
- Infinity Drawing (p. 128)

After Lunch	• Listen & Draw (p. 165)
	• Sky-Earth-Friend (p. 93)
	• Balancing Poses (p. 126)
Energizers	• 3-6-0 (p. 106)
	• Squats (p. 104)
	• Laughing Exercise (p. 148)
Calming & Centering	• Energy Ball (p. 122)
	• BrainScreen (p. 134)
	• HSP Breathing (p. 149)
	• Infinity Drawing (p. 128)
Memory Booster	• Bullfrog Belly Memory Game (p. 136)
	• BrainScreen (p. 134)
Mood Changer	• Push-ups (p.102)
	• Laughing Exercise (p. 148)
	• Compliment Game (p. 176)
Leadership	• I Have a Dream (p. 178)
	• Earth Challenges & Solutions (p. 189)

The above categories will be referenced for each of the thirty activities in Part 2.

The Brain Power 10 Essentials

Team Building

The strength of the team is each individual member.
The strength of each member is the team.
– Phil Jackson

You don't have to be a sports fan to have heard of the legendary basketball coach Phil Jackson, who is famous not only for his own storied basketball playing career, but for his unique coaching strategies that led to eleven NBA championship rings. What sports fans and other motivational leaders have learned from this man is that it is not only possible, but critical to take larger-than-life personalities such as Michael Jordan, Kobe Bryant, Dennis Rodman, and Shaquille O'Neil, among many others, and turn them into selfless team players. In lieu of their own self-interest, team players embrace the philosophy of harmony, authenticity, and respect for one another. In many respects, the process of team building in the classroom environment is the same. In Ilchi Lee's native Korean language, this is referred to as creating *Hap Shim* or "One Mind." There truly is no "I" in team, and the Brain Power Classroom is the perfect setting to drive this point home, by using the following exercises.

BENEFITS

- Improves morale and leadership skills

- Clearly defines objectives and goals

- Improves processes and procedures

- Improves team's productivity

- Identifies a team's strengths and weaknesses

- Improves the ability to problem solve

- Improves communication

There have been many recent developments in the understanding of the interconnectedness of the brains of friends and teammates. Using functional magnetic resonance imaging (fMRI) technology, University of Virginia researchers conducted a study that had participants undergo fMRI brain scans while threatening to give them electrical shocks, or give shocks to a friend. When the researchers threatened to shock a friend, the brain regions of the participants showed activity nearly identical to the ones displayed when the participant was personally threatened. "The correlation between self and friend was remarkably similar," said James Coan, coauthor of the study and a psychology professor at UVA's College of Arts & Sciences. "The finding shows the brain's remarkable capacity to model self to others; that people close to us become a part of ourselves."

From an evolutionary biology standpoint, we have learned that humans are built to connect on cognitive levels in relatively small groups of about 150 people of fewer. This makes sense, because humans initially developed small communities through harmonious collaboration for the collective good in order to sustain themselves more successfully.

Says Coan, "Threats can take things away from us. But

when we develop friendships, people we can trust and rely on who in essence become we [sic], then our resources are expanded, we gain. Your goal becomes my goal. It's a part of our survivability."

In short, our brains are social organs, which is what makes team building essential to developing a Power Brain. There is a plethora of research that shows that children learn better when they learn with the goal of teaching someone else rather than when they learn in preparation to take a test. Engagement in learning is a pro-social feature, and team building exercises expand and sustain students' abilities to tap their innate requirements for connection.

Through a variety of fun and challenging partner and small-group activities, Brain Power gives students valuable real-world experience in working with their peers. They learn to connect and interact in positive and empowering ways that improve communication and leadership skills. As personal relationships improve in the classroom, time on task and academic achievement increase.

On Fun Fridays, if the class finished everything it was supposed to, I promised to leave time for additional interactive Brain Power activities. After accolades were handed to students for a good week, I introduced the Wow Wow game, which challenged a team of two people to see how fast they could clap in sequence while keeping cadence. One week's Wow Wow competition involved Terrell and Garrison, a duo who couldn't seem to get along. They had gotten into several fights throughout the year, and I usually made a point to keep them as far apart from one another as possible. However, after my Brain Power workshop, I felt empowered to meet the conflict head on. I decided to make them partners. Once they started to mess up, I called to them, "Alright guys, you can do it; relax and breathe. Let me see it one more time."

I encouraged them until eventually the two boys made it to the finals. Garrison and Terrell were able to hold it together long enough until they actually beat out the other teams and won!

"So, how'd you guys win?" I asked, the other students looking on in awe. "Did you get along?"

"Yes," they answered in unison.

A bit smugly, I commented, "Thought you guys didn't like each other?"

Terrell and Garrison laughed and gave each other a fist bump. Through the Wow Wow game, they looked beyond their senseless battle in order to create a friendship that lasted the rest of the year.

The Exercises

The essence of team building is open-mindedness. If students are closed off or shut down, they cannot work together. The following exercises will inspire students by creatively breaking the ice, helping them have fun, and enabling more natural collaboration.

∞ THE NAME GAME

When to use it:	Energizer.
The goal/objective:	Students will creatively introduce themselves to their peers and support their classmates in order to create a successful team.
Considers national standards:	Statistics and probability, vocabulary acquisition and use.

INSTRUCTIONS

1. Invite students to form a circle.

2. One student begins by saying his or her name and creating a signature move or gesture to go with the introduction. For instance, Mary might say, "Hi, my name is Mary," while making jazz hands.

3. The rest of the class responds by using the name and movement. (E.g., "Hi, Mary [mimic jazz hands].")

4. Repeat the pattern with each student in the circle.

5. After each student has had a turn, ask for volunteers to remember at least three names and their corresponding movements until each student's name and movement has been recalled.

6. Go around the circle, this time asking the group to repeat in unison each student's name and movement. (E.g., "Hi, Kevin! [twirl]" "Hi, Sabrina! [Egyptian walk]" "Hi, Michelle! [diving pose]")

Extensions & modifications: Students can add a positive quality about themselves that begins with the same letter as their first name (e.g., Lucky Lou, Thoughtful Tanisha, Friendly Francesca). Students might also be encouraged to create a movement that demonstrates something about their personality, interests, or passions, such as a bat swing, if the student plays baseball. Challenge students to try to remember all of the names and movements in the class.

∞ SKY-EARTH-FRIEND

When to use it:	Morning routine, mood changer.
The goal/objective:	Students will coordinate and clap at least five times in sync with a partner, using different patterns.
Considers national standards:	Craft and structure, integration of knowledge and ideas, vocabulary acquisition and use.

INSTRUCTIONS

1. Invite students to form partners, standing back to back with legs a little wider than shoulder-width apart.

2. Clap hands one time above their heads while saying, "Sky."

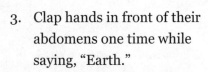

3. Clap hands in front of their abdomens one time while saying, "Earth."

4. Bending over and reaching through their legs, students meet their partner's two hands with a clap, while saying, "Friend."

5. Repeat five to ten times while remembering to smile.

Extensions & modifications: Students can move at a faster pace, change the sequence, or see how many times they can successfully complete the pattern without making a mistake.

∞ BALLOON CHALLENGE

Materials:	Requires one inflated balloon per team.
When to use it:	Energizer, mood changer.
The goal/objective:	Students will work with their team to pass a balloon around a circle following three rules.
Considers national standards:	Integration of knowledge and ideas, conventions of standard English.

INSTRUCTIONS

1. Invite the group to form a circle of eight to twelve students.

2. Hitting the balloon only one time, each student passes the balloon to the person directly to their left, so that the balloon travels clockwise around the circle. Students must follow three rules:
   - The balloon may not touch the floor.
   - Each student may only touch the balloon once per turn.
   - The balloon must travel clockwise and in order (a student may not hit the balloon out of turn).

3. The team gets a point for each time the balloon makes it all the way around the circle, back to the first student. The object is to see how many points the team can get.

4. Whenever the students break any of the rules, stop, discuss what went wrong, and strategize how to fix it for the next time.

Extensions & modifications: After a team has successfully made ten points, introduce a series of more challenging rounds. For Round 2, students may not hit the balloon with their dominant hand. For Round 3, students may not use either hand. For Round 4, students may not use the part of the body that was used by the student immediately prior to them. If the above format is too difficult, another variation is to have individuals or pairs of students count how many times they can hit the balloon without it touching the ground (giving a point for each time a student touches the balloon).

Physical Health

Physical fitness is not only one of the most important keys to a healthy body, it is the basis of dynamic and creative intellectual activity.
– John F. Kennedy

The school day can be long for teachers and students, and in-corporating physical activity to engage and reactivate the brain during a long lesson, after lunch, or on a rainy day is a key way to avoid slumps and sabotages. A recent report by the Centers for Disease Control and Prevention found that only 25 percent of American teenagers get enough daily physical exercise. Brain Power enables teachers to incorporate simple physical activities in the classroom setting that help our kids get their daily allow-ance of exercise.

The brain makes up only 2 percent of a person's body weight, but uses between 20 to 25 percent of the body's energy and oxygen intake. If we are to efficiently provide our brain the energy it requires to optimally perform consistently throughout the ebbs and flow of the day, it's important to replenish that en-ergy using brain breaks. Physical exercise is just one way we can

BENEFITS

- Increases blood flow to the brain
- Produces endorphins, "the happy hormones"
- Reduces cortisol, the stress hormone
- Makes you smarter

accomplish this—feeding and re-feeding a fatiguing brain in doses. Like a moving water wheel converting water into energy, moving our bodies fuels new nerve connections that are essential to brain health and function. Increasing heart rate and pushing more blood through the veins increases blood flow, especially to the extremities. The increased blood flow delivers needed oxygen, glucose, and other nutrients to the brain to help it function better.

The body is essentially the brain's connection to the outside world. A person's brain can have little effect on the surrounding environment if the rest of the body lacks strength and stamina.

Studies have shown that students who walked for twenty minutes before a test increased their problem-solving skills by ten percent and increased test scores. Movement also stimulates the production of hormones that combat stress and depression.

On the other hand, sitting for more than ten minutes reduces concentration and increases fatigue. A sluggish, tired body usually results in a sluggish, tired brain—while a strong, vibrant body houses—you guessed it—a strong, vibrant brain.

A growing body of research has convincingly proven that moving around every hour, even if for just one or two minutes, can help people dig themselves out of that 2:00 p.m. slump—when we crave a cup of coffee and our students' minds begin to wander. Other research urges people to take cues from their lack of concentration in order not to fall victim to it. When the mind begins to wander, getting up and moving around will ultimately make people more productive than if they would've tried to push through their haze.

Here are some simple exercises you can use in even the tightest of classroom spaces to boost the brain.

Derek, a fourth grader, was the prototypical "wiggler" who couldn't sit still for long, and his "sitting" usually involved half-way standing, leaning on his desk, rocking in his chair, etc. Although he was a bit small for his age, he was also extremely athletic and was always one of the first chosen to be on the basketball or kickball teams. He loved math but struggled with his multiplication tables. I knew that if he didn't improve his number sense and master his times tables, he couldn't succeed in what was to come in math. He'd grow more and more frustrated during his math assessments, would rarely finish tests on time, and made frequent avoidable mistakes.

In order to gain entry back into the classroom after lunch every day, each student had to solve a multiplication and/or division problem for me at the door. Derek hated doing this, and I noticed he would stand in the back of the line so as to not hold everyone else up by taking too long to solve his (significantly easier) mental math problem.

I had taught the Harmony Claps exercise as a simple coordination challenge, and my students loved it. One day, after all the other students had gained entry to the classroom, I held Derek back with me in the hall. "Derek, you know how you are so good at sports and Harmony Claps? Well, I want to try an experiment. I think Harmony Claps can help you solve your multiplication problems faster."

Derek wasn't convinced, but he was happy to give it a try.

I asked him to show me the Harmony Claps and he flew through the sequence easily, counting one through eight several times.

"Awesome. Now, I want you to try counting by twos."

Derek started again, not quite as fast this time, but made it through pretty well.

"Great! Now by threes."

He shot me a look. But Derek went through it, hesitating only once.

Derek noticed I was encouraged, and he followed suit. I said, "OK, Derek, now by fours; let's do it together. Four, eight . . . what comes next?"

I could see that Derek was still counting in his head to twelve, then sixteen, and onward. But I also noticed that he was counting faster, and he was smiling. When we got to the six times table, Derek balked. "Nah, Mr. Beal, it won't work."

"No problem, Derek. You did great. What's four times six?" I asked.

He froze.

"Why don't you try the Harmony Claps?"

He smiled again and solved it pretty quickly. I gave him a high five, and he entered the classroom. Each day after lunch, Derek and I would spend a minute using Harmony Claps to solve math problems, and I could see his confidence build. Soon, we had a math test. I had my head buried in a social studies textbook when, out of the corner of my eye, I saw Derek "sitting" in his seat, using the Harmony Claps exercise to solve his math problems.

He was careful not to make noise, mouthing the numbers as he silently clapped his hands over his head, in front of his chest, and under his legs. He got the answer and excitedly wrote it down. He looked up and gave me a smile and a knowing head nod. That's when it struck me: during the other math tests, Derek had been sitting passively, relatively still. Today, he was so excited that he was leaning forward, like he was running toward the next question. I kept watching, and, sure enough, every couple of minutes, Derek would perform the Harmony Claps exercise.

This solidified what I had already learned about multiple intelligence theory, specifically kinesthetic and musical intelligences. And, thanks to Derek's experience, I incorporated Harmony Claps (See Essential 3: Focus) into how I taught multiplication moving forward.

The Exercises

Kinesthetic learning is the absorption of information through physical movement. The following exercises, while all terrific energy burners, stress relievers, and physiological challenges, can be incorporated into lessons in order to teach students who learn better through carrying out activity.

PUSH-UP PROGRESS

When to use it:	Energizer, mood changer.
The goal/objective:	Students will increase stamina, gain strength, and increase number of push-ups over time.
Considers national standards:	Measurement and data, counting and cardinality, numbers and operations in base ten.

INSTRUCTIONS

1. Distribute Push-up Tracker Sheets (see Appendix).

2. Each morning, the students will do as many push-ups as they can and record the number on their forms. (Note: Students who cannot perform straight-leg push-ups can try knee push-ups and/or wall push-ups.)

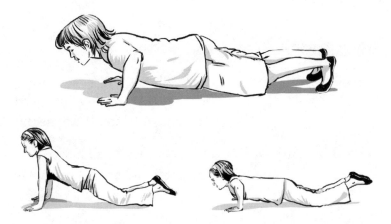

Extensions & modifications: Be sure to demonstrate proper push-up form (or have a student demonstrate). Place palms under the shoulders with elbows straight and legs extended back. Make a straight line from shoulders to heels. Flex the ankles with toes on the ground. When lowering the body, bend the elbows until they reach a ninety-degree angle.

SQUATS

When to use it:	Energizer.
The goal/objective:	Students will develop physical strength in the lower body while learning to center their energy.
Considers national standards:	Counting and cardinality, numbers and operations in base ten, integration of knowledge and ideas.

INSTRUCTIONS

1. Stand with feet in a parallel position, a little wider than shoulder-width apart, with arms straight in front at shoulder height parallel to the ground, neck and shoulders relaxed, tailbone curled under, and abdominal muscles engaged.

2. Gently bend the knees and lower the body into a sitting position, then go back to standing. That is one squat.

3. Repeat until the class has completed ten full squats.

4. Direct students to inhale through the nose and exhale out the mouth, keeping the neck and shoulders relaxed.

Extensions & modifications: Try doing this daily or weekly and monitor changes/improvements over time. You can use the Body & Brain Checkup Chart (see Appendix) as a guide, implementing a point system as an incentive:

- 1 point: less than ten squats
- 2 points: ten to twenty squats
- 3 points: twenty to thirty squats

(Add one point for each additional set of ten squats.) You can also guide students to do squats in pairs, facing their partner while holding hands and counting together with a smile.

3-6-0 BELLY DRUMMING

When to use it:	Morning routine, after lunch.
The goal/objective:	Students will create warmth in their body's energy center by patting the abdomen; students will build concentration through playing a fun and challenging rhythm-counting game.
Considers national standards:	Integration of knowledge and ideas, presentation of knowledge and ideas, conventions of standard English.

INSTRUCTIONS

1. Students form a circle.

2. Teach Belly Drumming—rhythmically tapping the abdomen below the navel with both palms while keeping the knees slightly bent. (Note: Explain the Water Up, Fire Down principle, see box.)

3. With each tap of their belly, one student at a time calls out numbers one to one hundred, moving clockwise around the circle.

4. When participants have a number that contains a 3, 6, or 0, they must jump rather than say the number aloud. (E.g., numbers one and two would be said aloud, the person who has three would jump instead; four and five

would be said aloud, and the person with six would jump. Seven, eight, and nine would be said aloud, and the person with ten would jump, and so on. From thirty to forty, all students would just jump and not say their number aloud; the same would be done for sixty to seventy.)

5. In the event the student calls out a number instead of silently jumping or jumps when they should call out a number, the student must say, "I am a Power Brain!" The group will encourage the student by giving them the "thumbs up" sign and responding, "Yes, you are!"

6. Begin again, starting at number one.

Extensions & modifications: Choose three different body motions, other than jumping, to represent the 3, 6, and 0. For example, you can raise one hand up for 3, both hands up for 6, and make a circular motion with hips for 0. For numbers with more than one target numeral in it, such as 30, 36, or 63, accompany each with two different motions.

Water Up, Fire Down

According to Eastern mind-body practices, our body's energy center is located in the lower abdomen. The core of our body is meant to be warm, and our head is meant to be cool. When our body is in a healthy state, warmth from the lower abdomen stimulates the kidneys, which sends water energy up our spine to the brain, cooling and refreshing the brain (keeping a cool head). When the fire energy flows down from the chest, the lower abdomen and intestines become warm and flexible (having a fire in the belly). When intense or prolonged stress occurs, this natural energy flow is disrupted, creating a heated brain. In order for the brain to be healthy, it has to remain cool. The state of Water Up, Fire Down optimizes brain activity, imparting vitality and the cool wisdom and judgment of a peaceful state of mind.

If the energy flow is reversed, with fire energy moving upward and water energy moving downward, the abdomen may become clammy and the neck and shoulders can become stiff. We feel frustrated and struggle to think clearly.

Water Up, Fire Down is a natural cycle that is found in other parts of nature, such as the process of photosynthesis. When you explain Water Up, Fire Down to your students, you can incorporate a lesson in photosynthesis. Consider how plants obtain their energy. They receive fire energy in the form of light from the sun. Their roots pull up water energy in the form of water from the ground. Water and light provide two of the raw materials necessary for photosynthesis, which turns these materials into a form of energy the plants can use. With this cycle of energy, plants and trees are able to grow and reproduce.

Focus

Concentrate all your thoughts upon the work at hand.
The sun's rays do not burn until brought to a focus.
– Alexander Graham Bell

On the first morning of fourth grade, Tommy charmingly shook my hand and said, "Pleased to meet you, Mr. Beal." It didn't take him long to manifest the behaviors I had been warned of by his third grade teacher and his mother. He was unfocused and lacked self-control and had been diagnosed with ADHD a few years prior.

In the very first small group brainstorming activity, Tommy was gone. I opened the door and saw Tommy happily pacing back and forth in the hallway outside my door. When he saw me, his face dropped, and he began to apologize, but added, "Because of my ADHD, I just can't help it. I promise it won't happen again."

I knelt down and smiled. "Tommy, I've got some important news for you." I waved my hand around his head like a magician. "I'm going to help you make your ADHD disappear."

BENEFITS

- Improved problem-solving abilities
- Clarity and self-awareness
- Stronger attention span
- Enhanced decision making
- Foundation for learning and higher-order thinking

"You are?! How?"

"This year, Tommy, you're going to learn how to use exercises to train your brain to focus. Do you know how to ride a bike?"

"Yes."

"Do you remember how at first you needed training wheels?"

"Yes, Mr. Beal."

"Well, you can think of your ADHD medicine as your training wheels. But, if you do your best and practice the exercises I show you everyday, you may be able to even take the training wheels off. How does that sound?"

"Great, Mr. Beal! My mom and I don't want me to take medicine anymore."

"I know, Tommy, she told me that. You'll see, Tommy, step by step, your Power Brain is going to get stronger and before you know it, you'll have the best focus in our class."

I have received objections about suggesting to Tommy that he can "cure" his ADHD through brain exercises. But I knew that if Tommy held onto that very strong preconception that he "couldn't focus," then he would continue following the same pattern. By telling him that our mental exercises would help him overcome his ADHD, I was assisting Tommy in opening his mind up to his potential. As the saying goes, "Good news creates a good brain." Some call it the placebo effect; "fake it until you make it;" or "mind over matter." I prefer, "If I say I can or I say I can't, I'm right either way."

From that moment, Tommy *loved* Brain Power, in particular, 3-6-0 Belly Drumming and Pinky-Thumb. I noticed that Tommy would be very focused after our exercises, but often only for a brief period before "zoning out" again. Tommy's arch nemesis was writing. His mother would write me notes explaining that Tommy would take hours to complete a simple paragraph in his reading response journal. When we had writing assignments in class, it was common for Tommy to "check out" and gloss over, avoiding the assignment altogether.

One day, however, I noticed Tommy fiddling under his desk. Only he wasn't fiddling—he was doing the Pinky-Thumb exercise. As I approached him, Tommy whispered, "Mr. Beal, this is helping me focus." I began giving Tommy time to go to the back of the room to practice 3-6-0 Belly Drumming or Push-up Progress to help refresh his focus. Whenever Tommy needed a break, he would simply get up, go to his spot in the room, do a quick exercise, and come back to his seat. This was the advent of the Brain Power Station that we recommend teachers designate in their classroom. As it turns out, the classroom wasn't his only station. Midway through the year, Tommy gave me a letter from his mother, which read:

"Mr. Beal, it is with happy tears in my eyes that I am writing you. It has now been exactly one month since Tommy's doctor agreed to take Tommy off his ADHD medication. I didn't tell you because I wanted to see how he would adjust in school. It's been a full month and—I can't believe I'm saying this—Tommy just finished all his homework in forty-five minutes. No meltdowns, no tantrums. He uses the exercises you showed him every day at home, and whenever he gets stuck, I see him inhaling and exhaling, whispering to himself, 'I can do it.' Mr. Beal, please keep up the excellent work. You have no idea what you have done for our family."

Tommy's story is a testament to the power of neuroplasticity. We implore our children to focus, be alert, and pay attention. However, in a world of digitized overstimulation and limited physical activity, we often fail to teach our students *how* to focus their attention. As discussed in previous chapters, the brain is an intricate system made up of 100 billion neurons with the mind-blowing ability to change and rewire, to make new connections every day. Tommy's brain didn't have to be stuck in the same firing-and-wiring patterns he had been conditioned to form, and he didn't have to justify his actions under a label of ADHD, which had become somewhat of a self-fulfilling prophesy.

This is not to say Tommy's symptoms were not valid or quite real; however, telling him something different, providing him an opportunity to think differently about himself, helped Tommy commit to the exercises. Tommy has stood as a prime example of how the elasticity of the brain, and focus in particular, can change patterns and futures.

The Exercises

The following activities help students integrate the left and right hemispheres of the brain for maximum focus. See Tip 25 "Persist Through Positivity" on page 80 for guidelines that help effectively teach these challenging mental flexibility exercises.

PINKY-THUMB

When to use it:	Transitions, morning routine.
The goal/objective:	Students will create new synapses by practicing to alternate movement of the pinky finger and thumb on each hand successfully. Students will smile, breathe out, and use positive self-talk to persevere through the challenge.
Considers national standards:	Key ideas and details, ratios, and proportional relationships.

INSTRUCTIONS

1. Make two fists and turn fists so the fingers face the chest.

2. Extend the pinky finger from the right fist and thumb from the left fist.

3. Pull the pinky and thumb back in.

4. Extend the right thumb and left pinky.

5. Switch again: right pinky and left thumb.

6. Continue alternating, building up speed and eventually switching both fingers simultaneously.

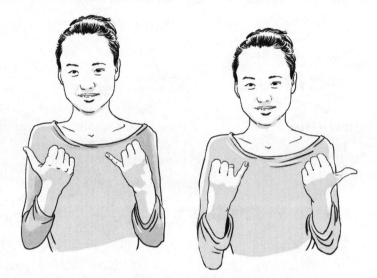

Extensions & modifications: Slowly switch one finger and one thumb at a time and work up to switching both in unison. Try to add singing a song, such as "Twinkle, Twinkle, Little Star," or any other well-known song with a repetitive rhythm. This will help students shift between the right and left fists more fluidly and with complete focus.

◎ HARMONY CLAPS

When to use it:	Transitions, morning routine.
The goal/objective:	Students will create new synapses by practicing a fun and challenging kinesthetic activity; students will practice math facts using exercise and rhythm.
Considers national standards:	Craft and structure, comprehension and collaboration, counting and cardinality.

INSTRUCTIONS

1. Clap hands in front of forehead while saying, "One."

2. Clap hands behind head while saying, "Two."

3. Clap hands in front of abdomen while saying, "Three."

4. Clap hands behind lower back while saying, "Four."

5. Lift right leg up and clap under raised knee while saying, "Five."

6. Clap hands in front of abdomen while saying, "Six."

7. Lift left leg up and clap under raised knee while saying, "Seven."

8. Clap hands in front of abdomen while saying, "Eight."

9. Repeat the above eight-clap pattern, slowly increasing the pace.

Extensions & modifications: Have students practice math facts by skip counting. Call out a number (1-12) and have students complete the Harmony Claps pattern counting by multiples of that number (i.e., for "6," they would count "6, 12, 18, 24," instead of "1, 2, 3, 4").

◎ WOW WOW (RHYTHM PARTNER CLAP)

When to use it:	Before a test, energizer.
The goal/objective:	Students will work with a partner to master a rhythm clapping game.
Considers national standards:	Numbers and operations in base ten, number systems, counting and cardinality.

INSTRUCTIONS

1. Have students stand up, choose a partner, and face each other.

2. Have students clap once in front of their chest and then once against their partner's palms saying, "Wow."

3. Next, they clap once in front of their chest and then twice against their partner's palms saying, "Wow, Wow," with each clap.

4. Again, they clap once in front of their chest and then three times against their partner's palms saying, "Wow, Wow, Wow."

5. Now, they clap once in front of their chest and then twice against their partners palms saying, "Wow, Wow."

6. And finally, they clap once in front of their chest and once on their partner's palms saying, "Wow."

7. Have the pair continue to follow the 1-2-3-2-1-2-3-2-1 pattern of clapping. See how long they can maintain the rhythm. For a challenge, have them increase their speed with each set.

Extensions & modifications: As the group improves their concentration, try having them circle up and use the same clapping pattern, but clapping the people's palms to their immediate right and left within the circle, rather than just one partner. Also, allow the students to create their own sounds for the game (i.e., animal sounds like "moo") to make it more fun. *Note:* The Wow Wow game is an excellent warm up before doing Energy Ball (see Essential 4: Mindfulness).

Mindfulness

The present moment is filled with joy and happiness.
If you are attentive, you will see it."
– Thích Nhất Hạnh

Numerous studies have verified mindfulness training's positive impact on overcoming depression and improving emotional regulation. Through mindfulness exercises, students access alpha brain waves, which helps them stay "in the zone" during assessments, thus enhancing their cognitive performance and academic achievement. Further, mindfulness training enhances emotional regulation, boosts immunity, and increases compassion. Most importantly, especially in the classroom, mindfulness controls stress and anxiety. Indeed, test anxiety is the number one reason students underperform on academic assessments. Therefore, Brain Education's mindfulness exercises are an invaluable tool to help proactively empower students to balance stress levels and focus on their academic tasks with a clear, confident mind.

As Thích Nhất Hạnh's beautifully simple quote reflects, being attentive to the present moment is the cornerstone of all mindfulness practices. Guiding students to being present in the moment and building their inner focus is the foundation for all learning, self-development, and self-mastery.

Indeed, the Ancient Greek aphorism, "know thyself," is the key to developing attributes such as concentration, emotional regulation, confidence, and intrapersonal intelligence.

Through mindfulness practices, such as the ones presented below, students learn to "know themselves" and develop the inner focus to overcome challenges and keep a positive focus on their goals.

If street smarts counted in school, Simone would've been at the top of the class. She was sarcastic and dismissive, an eye-roller who sucked her teeth when she disliked something I said. But, on the rare occasion when she'd let down her guard and smile, she could melt my heart.

However smart and capable, Simone struggled academically in all her core subjects and was devastated when she had to repeat fifth grade as a Level 1 (significantly below standards) in English language arts and math.

At the beginning of the year, the class took a New York State exam pre-test in social studies, and, as expected, Simone put her head down when the test began, refusing to take it. When I went over to her, she had tears in her eyes and said, "Why should I bother taking this? We both know I'm going to fail." Then, overcome with anger, she swept the papers off her desk and put her head back down.

What helped Simone was the mindfulness practice called Energy Ball, in which students close their eyes and visualize the formation of a ball of energy between their hands. I kept encouraging Simone and the others to try their best, reminding them that mistakes are okay and that giving their best was the only thing I was counting on. Using the Energy Ball practice on a daily basis, I began to see significant changes in Simone's attitude.

When the April New York State English language arts exam was administered, complete with over thirty pages of multiple choice, short answer, and full essay response questions, it was easy to feel overwhelmed. I gave Simone a reassuring wink, and she whispered to me, "I got this, Mr. Beal." As I proctored the exam, I noticed Simone take a break and close her eyes. I knew she was creating her energy ball because it was followed by a brief smile and slow breaths, just as I taught her.

When she turned in the test, I asked her how she did. "It was tough," she answered. "But I did alright. I did what you told me. I kept seeing myself getting the right answer. I did my best."

Simone not only raised her performance to a high Level 2 (approaching standards), she proudly graduated fifth grade with her classmates.

The Exercises

These Brain Power mindfulness practices use meditation, visualization, balance, breathing, and guided imagery to help students create alpha brain waves to promote inner focus and relaxed concentration.

⊙ ENERGY BALL

When to use it:	Before a test, calming and centering.
The goal/objective:	Students will use relaxed concentration to create and sustain energetic sensations between their hands. **Note:** Having students practice the Wow Wow activity (see Essential 3: Focus) is an excellent warmup before Energy Ball as it helps stimulate the students' palms so that they can sense energy faster.
Considers national standards:	Movement forms, movement concepts.

INSTRUCTIONS

1. Ask your students if they are familiar with characters who "shoot" energy from their hands (Pokemon, Naruto, Dragon Ball Z, Avatar, etc.). Explain that in this activity we will be using our focus to create our own energy ball.

Tell them that following three simple guidelines will help them focus: 1) Sitting up straight; 2) Not talking during the activity (we will share at the end); and 3) Closing your eyes to tune out distractions.

2. Begin by doing several sets of rhythmic clapping to warm up the hands, or try Power Brain Clapping (p. 75) or the Wow Wow activity (p.117).

3. Ask students to sit comfortably with their backs straight and shoulders relaxed, and breathe deeply, inhaling through the nose and exhaling from the mouth.

4. Have them tap their fingertips together (up to one hundred times), focusing on the vibration occurring in the fingertips.

5. Guide them to stop tapping slowly, close their eyes, and focus on the space between their palms; students may feel warm, soft, tingling, or magnetic sensations between their hands.

6. Guide their visualization, asking students to imagine holding a ball of energy in their hands. Slowly rotate this energy ball, making semicircles and rotating the opposite way.

7. As they inhale, have them slowly stretch the energy ball bigger; on the exhale, have them bring their hands closer, making the energy ball smaller. (Repeat several times.)

8. Have them allow the energy ball to divide into two parts, holding one in the palm of each hand. Guide them to feel the weight of the energy in each palm.

9. Guide them to slowly allow the energy ball in one hand to become heavier, imagining it becoming hard to hold. And let the other energy ball become lighter, feeling it floating away. Slowly switch, heavy and light, and feel the difference. (Repeat several times.)

10. Have them gently bring their hands back to facing each other, and feel the energy ball come back together and be even stronger. Let the energy ball move any way that it wants, any motion will do. Keep focusing on the palms as the energy guides the movement.

11. Have them slowly bring their energy ball down to their body's energy center (lower abdomen). Hold for three seconds. Rest the palms on the abdomen, transferring the energy into the belly.

12. Take three deep breaths, filling up the abdomen, and feel the energy transfer through the belly.

Extensions & modifications: Some students will not appear to be focused (e.g., eyes are open, bodies fidgety, etc.). Like adults, they need to practice concentrating and visualizing. Try having them focus on the colors they see in their energy ball, the textures, etc. Encourage students to close their eyes and try again. With practice, they will become more comfortable. Always allow time for students to share their experiences at the end. Additionally, students can draw pictures of what their energy ball looked like—an incentive for students who had difficulty the first time to focus on and remember the ball's characteristics the next time they participate in the activity.

BALANCING POSES

When to use it:	Before a test, after lunch, calming and centering.
The goal/objective:	Students will engage their inner focus to improve their balance and concentration.
Considers national standards:	Integration of knowledge and ideas, vocabulary acquisition and use.

INSTRUCTIONS

1. Stand up and spread out, allowing each student personal space, with palms together in front of the chest.

2. Slowly lift one leg, bending the knee ninety degrees with the toe pointed down and close to the standing leg, like a flamingo.

3. Have the group hold this flamingo pose for ten counts.

4. Keeping the knee up, turn it out to the side, and extend arms out to the sides like the branches of a tree. Hold this tree pose for another ten counts. (If there isn't enough space, students can alternatively keep their palms touching and raise their hands over their head.)

5. Extend the lifted leg behind the body and hinge the body forward at the waist, arms remaining out to the side, to create an airplane pose. Hold for ten counts.

6. Switch legs and repeat—flamingo, tree, plane.

Extensions & modifications: Once the students become familiar with this series of balancing poses, have them try them with their eyes closed. See if they can work up to holding each position for thirty seconds or a minute. To practice mindfully, try leading the Energy Ball activity first and having them visualize their energy ball turning into an "Energy Tower" that holds their body upright even when their eyes are closed.

INFINITY DRAWING

When to use it:	Before a test, after lunch, calming and centering.
The goal/objective:	Students will relax their brain waves and connect with their inner rhythm by continuously tracing the infinity sign. Students will challenge themselves by tracing the infinity with their non-dominant hand.
Considers national standards:	Key ideas and details, geometry, analysis, inquiry, and design.

INSTRUCTIONS

1. Give each student two sheets of paper with an infinity template (or draw the infinity sign on the board and have them draw their own on the paper). Ask students to color in a dot in the middle of the infinity symbol, where the lines intersect. Encourage them to keep focusing their relaxed gaze on the dot as they go through this exercise.

2. On one sheet of paper, have students trace the infinity sign using their dominant writing hand. Guide them to trace at least thirty times. Remind them to relax their body and breathe comfortably as they make a rhythm.

3. On the other sheet of paper, guide students to trace the infinity sign using their less dominant hand. Remind them to 1) smile; 2) breathe out through their mouth;

and 3) tell themselves, "My brain loves challenges!" Guide them to relax their body and make a rhythm, even though it may feel initially awkward using their less dominant hand.

4. Discussion: "Which hand made it easier to complete the activity?" "In what way do you feel different after the activity?"

Extensions & modifications: Challenge students to trace more challenging shapes with both hands. They can also draw any lines or forms freely and continuously, with their own flow or rhythm, without picking up their writing implement.

Memory

Memory is a muscle, to be exercised and improved.
– Joshua Foer

For many years, brain scientists were certain that the brain was not capable of making new nerve cells to replace lost ones. But evidence now shows that the brain can produce new nerve cells (a process called neurogenesis) in some areas of the brain related to memory. In addition, research shows that prolonged stress negatively impacts the hippocampus, the region of the brain that regulates memory.

Brain Education helps improve memory by reducing stress, making the learning process fun and engaging, and providing a nurturing environment for students to feel safe, happy, and loved. The exercises that follow teach students how to picture the information they hear in their mind's eye, which we call BrainScreen Visualization (see exercise on p. 134), as well as stimulate students' memory by giving them ownership over a task or activity they have just learned or done, thereby imprinting it permanently.

BENEFITS

- Boosts brain functionality
- Trains visual memory
- Increases long-term memory
- Prevents memory-related illnesses
- Helps keep focus and practice patience
- Increases attention span

Elizabeth studied hard, participated enthusiastically in class discussions, and always had a great attitude. But when it came time to take tests, she consistently underperformed, particularly in English language arts. While her essay responses lacked detail, I knew it wasn't an issue of effort, so I addressed her comprehension.

Working with Elizabeth after school to help her "remember stuff better," I introduced her to Brain-Screen Visualization. Instead of reading and discussing a passage, we gave her memory a "workout." She liked that idea.

I read to her a list of ten random words (frog, horse, ice cream, blanket, etc.), and when I finished, Elizabeth wrote down the words she could remember in the order she had heard them. The first time, she got five out of ten right, which is a fairly low score, and she had the order of the words mixed up. I asked her what strategy she used to remember the words, to which she answered, "I don't know. It's like they're all just floating in my mind, and I try to grab them."

Next, I told her we would try the same exercise, only we would do the Energy Ball exercise (p. 122) first to help her concentrate, followed by the creation of a BrainScreen on which she would visualize the words as I called them out, as if she were creating her own mental movie. On the next try, Elizabeth improved, getting seven of the ten words correct. She was noticeably excited and encouraged about her marked and immediate progress. We met twice a week for a month to practice building her memory. By our eighth and final afterschool session, Elizabeth could visualize and recall twenty-nine of the thirty words I had read to her in the order I had read them.

Moving forward, when Elizabeth read a passage, she created a mental movie that detailed the events of what she was reading. It was common during an exam to see Elizabeth with her eyes closed, using her Brain-Screen to recall details from the story and to visualize her response before putting pencil to paper. Her ELA test score improved from Level 2 to Level 3. With her increased confidence and ability not to get discouraged, Elizabeth's writing became more fluid, and she even began to challenge herself in reading a variety of works.

The Exercises

We are three times more likely to remember what we see and hear than what we just hear. The following exercises focus on teaching students techniques to visualize in their mind's eye what they are hearing as they hear it as a way to increase long-term memory, an asset necessary when being tested on something in April that was taught months prior.

BRAINSCREEN VISUALIZATION

When to use it:	Memory booster, morning routine, at the end of a lesson to help students "save" the information in their brains.
The goal/objective:	Students will practice visualizing aural information, creating relevant connections, and saving mental images using their BrainScreen.
Considers national standards:	Key ideas and details, presentation of knowledge and ideas, vocabulary acquisition and use.

INSTRUCTIONS

1. Explain to your students that we all have a BrainScreen, like a mental movie screen, that we can create through our imagination. Guide students to close their eyes and warm up the BrainScreen by imagining a screen, like

a large movie screen or a three-dimensional tablet, in front of their forehead.

2. Call out an image and instruct students to visualize it on their BrainScreens. Image ideas can include a frog, volcano, ballet dancer, eagle, basketball player, monkey, astronaut, cloud, etc.

3. Now that the BrainScreen is open and warmed up, guide students to picture themselves on their BrainScreen and pretend they are the star of their own movie. Guide them to visualize themselves when they were learning a lesson you had taught recently; picture every detail.

4. Students can then focus on their favorite part of the lesson. Ask: "What does your brain remember?" "Can you see it on your BrainScreen?"

5. If time allows, have students share or draw a picture of what they saw on their BrainScreens.

6. Process the activity by asking, "How did it feel to use your BrainScreen?" "How can this help you in school? At home? In your life?"

Extensions & modifications: This technique can be incorporated into your curriculum by inviting students to use their BrainScreens to recreate a scene from a book, history lesson, or a science or mathematical concept.

BULLFROG BELLY

When to use it:	Before a test, memory booster, morning routine.
The goal/objective:	Students will practice "working out" their memory while strengthening their body's core and improving energy circulation through this kinesthetic activity.
Considers national standards:	Knowledge of language, vocabulary acquisition and use.

INSTRUCTIONS

1. Review the Water Up, Fire Down principle of energy circulation. Explain that one exercise to create heat in the lower abdomen is Bullfrog Belly. Have them visualize a bullfrog (or show them a picture), and envision it expanding and contracting its vocal sac. Explain that in this exercise, we expand and contract our abdomen to create heat and strength in our energy center.

2. Stand with feet a little wider than shoulder-width apart, with neck and shoulders relaxed.

3. Bend the knees slightly, about forty-five degrees.

4. Place both palms on the abdomen.

5. While continuing to breathe normally, students extend their bellies out as far as they can and then withdraw in toward the spine as far as possible. This is one repetition.

6. Each student takes a turn counting aloud for ten repetitions. Once the tenth repetition is reached, the student shares a favorite color.

7. When the next student counts to ten, that student is to recall the previous color while adding his or her favorite color.

8. Continue this pattern, counting and adding colors, until each student has had a chance (e.g., if there are twenty students, the last person to count will need to recall the colors added by the previous nineteen students. Having the group help as the list gets longer encourages teamwork and creates a positive group dynamic).

Extensions & modifications: Once the group gets used to this exercise, change topics, inviting students to share a favorite food, game, country, or city. Use topics from class curriculum, such as names of poets, historical figures, vocabulary words, literary genres, continents, etc.

⊙ SPEED BRAIN

When to use it:	Memory booster.
The goal/objective:	Students practice using relaxed concentration to scan a visual image to strengthen their memory.
Considers national standards:	Print concepts, comprehension and collaboration, knowledge of language.

INSTRUCTIONS

1. Give each student a sheet of blank paper and writing implement.

2. Share a series of images with them (use the Speed Brain graphic in the Appendix), allowing students ten seconds to imprint each image on their BrainScreens before the image is removed.

3. Students draw the images they remember on their sheets of paper.

4. Discussion: How well did the students do? What helped them remember the images? What strategies can they use

to allow their brains to absorb the images? How can this help in school, at home, and/or in life?

Extensions & modifications: Begin with fewer images and increase up to sixteen. To help them improve, guide students to relax their eyes and use their peripheral vision to take in the whole of the image, as if they are using a printer to scan the image. As they relax their eyes and trust their brain, they will gradually improve. As they improve, have the students challenge themselves by adding more images and giving them less time for observation.

Emotional Wellness

It is not the strongest of the species that survives, nor the most intelligent that survives. It is the one that is the most adaptable to change.
– Charles Darwin

Reacting impulsively to situations, being burdened by too much stress, and allowing emotional highs and lows to sweep them away can prevent students from making good choices in and about their lives. Emotional regulation is critical for self-value, good habit formation, integrity, goal achievement, and positive relationships. While research indicates that moderate stressors can improve short-term performance in both children and adults, uncoordinated and repeated activations of the stress system can injure both body and brain. Too much stress, especially when stemming from emotional upset, can increase cortisol levels and decrease blood flow and oxygen to the brain. In the school setting, anxiety is a chief cause of student underperformance, while stress is a prime contributor to educator burnout. Additionally, roughly 80 percent of modern physical ailments have been identified as stress-related.

BENEFITS

- Teaches self-care, relaxation, stress reduction, and the cultivation of inner strength
- Inspires more productive emotional expression
- Helps form supportive and interdependent relationships with others
- Self-awareness and personal growth

Emotions that cause stress have a huge impact on brain chemistry. Stress hormones can literally shrink brain cells, while endorphins—the "happy chemicals" released from positive emotions—are proven to enhance brain functioning.

Brain Education, particularly in the emotional wellness realm, relies on training exercises that release stress, frustration, anxiety, physical energy, and emotional charge—demonstrating to students that emotions are changeable. Students learn that emotions are things people can control, rather than things that just randomly happen to them. Students begin to see the relationship between the body and stress and how to use physical exercises to manage their emotions effectively. The ultimate goal is to help students become centered, especially when facing challenges, and make healthy choices for their lives.

Identify → Accept → Release → Create

First, Brain Education helps students **identify** their emotions and understand that the many different emotions we all feel are temporary states that can be changed. These emotions are not who we are. While we experience a range of emotions, they do not define who we are, what we stand for, and how we live. We do not need to attach to our emotions, especially the negative ones. Instead, we guide students to simply **accept** the emotions they are feeling. When we can accept our emotions honestly, they begin to lessen their grip on us, and we can ask ourselves, "Do I want to keep this emotion or change it?" When we want to change our emotion, we **release** the negative emotion through exercise. Finally, when we partake in happy actions (like laughing, singing, dancing, etc.), we **create** happiness. Through taking an action, we change the way we feel. By following this pattern of identifying, accepting, releasing, and creating, we are able to choose our emotions and work consciously to feel the way that we want to feel.

In the fall of 2015, I had the honor of leading a successful pilot program for 180 at-risk middle school students in District 7 of the South Bronx. (You will read about two students who participated in this pilot, Shauna and Jeffrey, in later Essentials.) Corresponding with a citywide initiative to promote social-emotional wellness by Chancellor Carmen Fariña and under the expert leadership of Superintendents Yolanda Torres and Elisa Alvarez, we were able to help these students make significant changes in their academic and personal lives.

District 7 is the poorest socioeconomic district in New York City, and many of the students deal with a variety of lifestyle stressors that make learning difficult. As you'll read in the case of Shauna and Jeffrey, the students initially met our Brain Power leadership program with resistance and distrust, but through the sincere guidance of my team and the district staff that we trained in Brain Power, the students quickly let down their walls. And, just as I shared in the story in this book's Introduction regarding how push-ups helped Terrell and Devante neutralize their anger, we observed amazing transformations in how the students regulated their emotions. As you can see in the graph below, over the eight-week pilot program, negative emotional indicators decreased by an average of 65 percent, while pro-social behaviors increased by 50 percent.

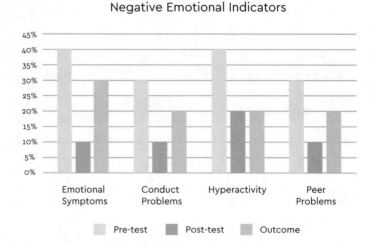

Brain Power's Impact on Negative Emotional Indicators

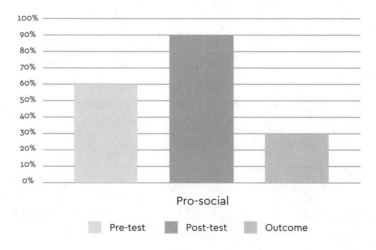

Brain Power's Impact on Pro-Sociality

On December 10, 2015, the district held a celebration to showcase what the students had learned about themselves and honor their progress. That night, we heard moving testimonials from Superintendent Alvarez, educators, parents, and students, including:

"Brain Power helped me learn to control myself and to stay calm. I was also really shy, but being with people doing stuff that was actually pretty fun (especially in the camp) helped me. Now I'm not as scared as I was before to talk to new people and try new things."
Angelica, student, Middle School 29

"I don't know what you are doing at these workshops, but whatever you are doing is working. My daughter and I used to argue a lot, and she would have outbursts, but since she has been doing Brain Power, she is able to step away, regroup, and come back and have a conversation with me. Keep up the good work."
Luz, parent, Intermediate School 151

"Brain Power made me feel that I could be myself. Brain Power made me feel that I have a family. I feel confident and can speak what is in my mind."
Jocelyn, student, Junior High School 162

The Two Principles of Emotional Wellness

1. "My emotions are not me; they are *mine*."
2. "Happy actions create happiness," meaning, "I can change my mood."

The Exercises

In addition to releasing strong emotions, the following exercises teach students how to choose the emotions that are helpful to a given situation, task, or relationship. They also learn how to take happy actions in order to create happiness.

💗 EMOTIONAL INVENTORY

When to use it:	Mood changer.
The goal/objective:	Students will identify, compare, evaluate, and discuss various emotions that they feel.
Considers national standards:	Range of reading and level of text complexity, range of writing, knowledge of language.

INSTRUCTIONS

1. Give each student a copy of the Emotions List (see Appendix).

2. Students write an example of when they have felt each listed emotion.

3. Ask students to share examples. What are the similarities and/or differences they share with other classmates? What emotion feels best? Why? What does this tell us about emotions?

4. On a separate blank piece of paper, students make a list of the various emotions or feelings they have experienced today.

5. Ask the students to share. What are the similarities and/ or differences they share with other classmates? What is their favorite emotion and why?

6. Guide students to understand that we all feel many different emotions and that emotions are temporary states that we have the power to change, if we choose to.

Extensions & modifications:
Explore the range of emotions by reacting with facial expressions in response to emotions being called out. Students may choose to react using their entire bodies, or explore their range of emotions through illustrations, facial expressions, and writing short scenes in which they act out an experience.

🫀 LAUGHING EXERCISE

When to use it:	Mood changer, energizer.
The goal/objective:	Students practice laughing as an exercise to demonstrate the principle: "Happy actions create happiness."
Considers national standards:	Key ideas and details, conventions of standard English, knowledge of language.

INSTRUCTIONS

1. Encourage students to spread out for some personal space.

2. Take a few deep breaths, inhaling through the nose and exhaling from the mouth while smiling.

3. Invite students to laugh as hard as they can for one full minute without stopping, and join them in the exercise. Even if nothing is perceivably funny, encourage all students to use 100 percent of their energy for their laughing.

4. After a minute, survey the group: "How many of you feel lighter? Calmer? More focused?" "Did laughing become easier? Did your laughter feel more genuine?" "Do you think you were laughing in response to a classmate's laughter?" "How do you think this affected your body?"

Extensions & modifications: Laughter is contagious, so if students feel awkward, self-conscious, or strange at first, offer them multiple opportunities to try.

♡ HSP (HEALTH SMILE PEACE) BREATHING

When to use it:	Mood changer, after lunch, calming and centering.
The goal/objective:	Students will practice letting go of negative thoughts and emotions and embracing a positive mindset.
Considers national standards:	Key ideas and details, text types and purposes, knowledge of language.

INSTRUCTIONS

1. Display the HSP Smile picture (see Appendix). (Alternatively, have students close their eyes and imagine a friend or loved one smiling.)

2. Guide students to imitate the smile.

3. With closed eyes, guide students to imagine they are sitting under a waterfall of golden energy. As they breathe in, this bright, positive light refreshes their brain.

4. As they exhale through their mouth, have students imagine negative emotions releasing from their brain. With each breath, their brain gets brighter, lighter, and happier.

5. Repeat several times.

Extensions & modifications: Once students have completed HSP Breathing, they can visualize the day that they want to create. This is an excellent activity for after lunch in that it invites students to let go of any negative thoughts from the morning and focus with a bright, positive mindset on their goals for the afternoon ahead.

Confidence

Without a humble but reasonable confidence in your own powers, you cannot be successful or happy.
– Norman Vincent Peale

Numerous scientific studies have confirmed what every teacher intuitively knows: When our students believe in their abilities and have confidence in themselves, they are more apt to be successful. Indeed, self-efficacy—students' beliefs that they will be successful in a given task—is a powerful determinant of positive outcomes.

Brain Power activities build confidence by presenting challenging tasks, both mental and physical, that students cannot initially master, while guiding them to overcome their limitations as they practice. Their root, Brain Education, applies the neuroscientific principle of neuroplasticity to understand that confidence—like all other attributes—is not fixed, but rather can be cultivated through training. Through "confident actions"—self-declaration, HSP Gym, and other Brain Power activities—students create a more confident mindset.

When Shauna first began Brain Power, it was part of the leadership program we held at Junior High School 162 in the Bronx. At only twelve years old, Shauna's teachers had identified her as painfully shy and already a follower, which is what led them to recommend her for the program.

Not trusting herself enough to fit in based on her own strengths, and not confident enough to notice what those strengths even were, Shauna sought approval from her peers by going along with whatever they did or said, especially when they skewed negative. If the girls paid too much attention to the boys, Shauna distracted herself with them as well. If someone's behavior was of the bullying nature, impolite, or nasty, Shauna would laugh in agreement instead of defend the victims or correct the bad behavior.

Not all shyness comes from a lack of confidence, but in Shauna's case, it did. Her low self-esteem affected her self-identity, until she turned outward to determine who she was, instead of meeting the true Shauna within. She lacked the ability to gauge when she did something right or wrong, and looked for outside validation, mostly in the form of physical attention from boys.

As I led the group through some team building exercises in the gymnasium, Shauna didn't say a word nor make eye contact with me or her peers. Shauna didn't ask or assume why she was there; in fact, she seemed pretty apathetic to the entire experience. We began with less personal activities like flying eagle poses and progressed to challenging balance poses with closed eyes. She seemed to be interested in lengthening the time she could keep a pose with her eyes closed, because each time she'd topple over, she would try again. She had an inner-competitiveness that was being ignited and challenged.

Initially, when we practiced the Balloon Challenge game (see Essential 1: Team Building), Shauna wouldn't speak during the activity, unenthusiastically batting the balloon to the person next to her. But as the group let the balloon fall to the floor, losing the game, she took more of a responsibility to keep the balloon from falling, acquiescing to the necessity of collaborating with the other students.

One of our later activities was the Compliment Game (see Essential 9: Character), after which I noticed Shauna begin to identify her strengths and connect to personal goals that allowed her confidence to grow. She became more demonstrative in sharing what she thought her own talents were, when before, she drew blanks. At first, she held her head low and cowered when people complimented her, but by the end of the program, she learned to acknowledge and accept the compliment, sincerely saying, "Thanks!"

Back in her classroom, her teachers noted that Shauna was beginning to lead by example rather than follow. She spoke up if others were negative, and most importantly, she saw her pattern for looking for approval from others, particularly boys, and chose not to let them deter her from creating more positive goals.

The Exercises

These exercises reinforce the mind-body principle of "Where your mind (attention) goes, energy follows," as they explicitly guide students to brainstorm their positive attributes while focusing on their inner strengths.

CONFIDENT QUALITIES

When to use it:	Mood changer.
The goal/objective:	Students will identify and discuss their personal strengths to gain confidence in themselves, while supporting and reinforcing their classmates' positive attributes.
Considers national standards:	Range of reading and level of text complexity, production and distribution of writing.

INSTRUCTIONS

1. Brainstorm with students and share aloud what it means to be confident.

2. Ask students to write five of their own strengths or good qualities they feel confident about on a sheet of paper. Use phrases beginning with, "I am." (E.g., "I am smart," "I am athletic," "I am generous.")

3. Invite students to share their lists with the class or within their small group.

4. Students should reinforce each other by responding, "Yes, you are," and giving a thumbs-up after their classmate has read all of his or her phrases.

5. Discussion: "What strengths or good qualities does the group have in common?" "Are there any strengths or good qualities that we would like to develop further?" "How did it feel to support your group?"

Extensions & modifications: Students can create physical motions or gestures to accompany their declarations. Other students can repeat the movement or gesture while saying, "Yes, you are!" If students are struggling for brainstorming ideas, invite them to think about someone who inspires them, like a popular historical leader, a parent, teacher, clergy member, sports figure, and so on, and define their strength or positive characteristic. Ask, "Why do these people inspire you?" "What strengths or positive qualities do they possess?"

Students may also act out what they think confidence looks like. Encourage them to use their entire bodies with 100 percent of their energy and enthusiasm. Discuss: "What is confident body language versus insecure body language?"

"How does it feel to be in a confident stance rather than a shy or insecure stance?"

Older students might enjoy watching social psychologist Amy Cuddy's TED Talk about the effects of "power posing," and how changing body language changes the chemistry of the brain, further supporting the principle of "happy action creates happiness."

⭐ SELF-DECLARATION

When to use it:	Mood changer, energizer.
The goal/objective:	Students will build intrapersonal intelligence by practicing self-reflection, students will confidently share their self-declaration with their classmates.
Considers national standards:	Integration of knowledge and ideas, conventions of standard English, knowledge of language, creativity and innovation.

INSTRUCTIONS

1. Guide students to sit up straight, with shoulders relaxed, eyes closed, and focus on breathing in through the nose and out from the mouth.

2. Students should open their BrainScreens to focus on the question, "Who am I?"

3. Guide students to remain focused on their breathing as they continue silently asking themselves the question. Guide them to go beyond more superficial answers (their name, gender, age, nationality, etc.) to focus on their inner character.

4. Once students have their answers, ask them to share their declaration out loud using a definitive sentence, such as, "I am strong," "I am kind," or "I am intelligent."

Extensions & modifications: If time allows, invite students to create an illustration of what they saw on their BrainScreens to accompany their declaration. Advanced students might wish to write short responses.

If students struggle finding an answer, suggest that they pick their favorite "Confident Quality." For a more powerful effect, invite students to the front of the class to shout their declaration. Classmates will reply, "Yes, you are!" to which the declarer confirms by responding, "Yes, I am!"

✳ HSP (HEALTH SMILE PEACE) GYM

When to use it:	Calming and centering, mood changer.
The goal/objective:	Students will connect with their inner confidence by holding a challenging isometric breathing posture.
Considers national standards:	Understanding challenges, physical fitness, creativity and innovation, information literacy, flexibility and adaptability.

INSTRUCTIONS

1. Students stand with feet shoulder-width apart; neck and shoulders are relaxed with knees bent to about forty-five degrees.

2. Students should open their arms wide to the side and flex their hands, elbows slightly bent.

3. Guide them to close their eyes and focus on breathing and holding the pose while smiling.

4. Remind students of their Self-Declaration and/or Confident Quality. Encourage them to feel the inspiration from this attribute, and feel the corresponding strength in their body when they focus on this positive trait.

5. Have them hold the pose for five to ten minutes or as time allows.

6. Offer encouragement by telling students, "You are strong," "You are confident," "Keep smiling."

7. Discuss: "How do you feel now?" "How did your energy level change when you focused on your Self-Declaration?" "What did you learn about yourself through this activity?"

Examples & modifications: Challenge students to hold the pose longer each time. Always guide them to process the impact the quality of their thoughts (positive or negative) had on their ability to complete the exercise.

Creativity

Imagination is more important than knowledge.
– Albert Einstein

Of all the Essentials, creativity is my favorite. Not because it is more important than any of the others, but because it is the bedrock of every other Essential—the thread running through all the Brain Power activities. Consider that we cannot be good leaders, become mindful, achieve physical fitness, possess focus, nor make a commitment to emotional wellness without tapping creative ways in which to develop the methods, carve out the time to hone them, and elevate and challenge our aptitude.

Every human being is a creative genius. Most people may doubt that statement, but I truly believe it. I believe it because of one special attribute of the human being—the human brain. The human brain is a creation machine, constantly producing thoughts, ideas, perceptions, solutions, and beliefs. But it is also true that many people never live up to this potential. We start to believe that we are not one of the talented few who are destined for greatness, and we settle into conventional lives instead.

As educators, we should help our students believe in their creative potential. If our children don't believe in themselves,

BENEFITS

- Creativity breeds adaptability and resilience
- Represents higher order thinking skills
- Provides an engaging atmosphere of intrinsic motivation
- Engages a multitude of learning styles and intelligences
- Encourages self-expression, innovation, and introspection

it's hard for them to express their creativity. Creativity and confidence goes hand in hand. Always remind them they can do anything if they truly choose it and act upon it, because their brains are so amazing.

Creativity was the impetus behind Ilchi Lee's development of Brain Education through his own creative spirit and the honing of creative skills in students in his native South Korea. The growth of Brain Education happened organically, and its curriculum was created by a community of students and teachers who were fueled by the effectiveness of creativity in learning, feeling, and doing. For instance, I mentioned in an earlier section that the Brain Power Station of my classroom grew out of a need for one of my students to retreat and collect himself privately, which is just one way Brain Education has been creatively directed and enhanced by its participants' needs and natural behaviors.

However, what I think most surprises people about creativity is that it transcends the idea of artistry. I have witnessed creativity's usefulness in the most impactful, intimate, and vulnerable way, by helping children picture bright futures without collapsing under the burden of reality, even when that reality is the sudden tragic death of a young classmate.

When Class 506 lost Patrice to an undiagnosed heart condition, he was only eleven years old. To say children and adults alike were incapable of processing the shock, tragedy, and grief of such news is an understatement. Helping my students navigate these raw emotions was one of the most challenging things I had ever faced. Thanks to my early exposure to Brain Education and a generous offer from a musician friend of mine, our class was able to write and record a tribute song and perform it for the school and Patrice's family.

I went first, writing my verse about what I remembered most about Patrice, what I admired, and how kind he was. You will read more about Patrice in Essential 10: Citizenship, and see just what a selfless boy he was. My verse modeled self-expression to my students, and with the help of my producer friend putting my lyrics to music, I was able to guide some of Patrice's closest friends to write verses too, while the rest of the class joined in to write and sing the chorus.

Patrice we want to thank you for being our friend/
and we're sad that we're not gonna see you again/
but your memory will always live on/
and we'll think about you every time we sing this song/
I got water in my eyes, my tears will never end/
Patrice you were so special, a really special friend.

Through the creative and imaginative process of writing and performing our song, our class was also able to: promote team building through creative collaboration (Essential 1), stay focused enough to write an entire song (Essential 3), use mindfulness to sit with our pain and process it through words (Essential 4), memorize the song lyrics (Essential 5), induce a state of emotional wellness (Essential 6), exude confidence when performing in front of the entire school (Essential 7), be creative (Essential 8), demonstrate good character in honoring a classmate's life (Essential 9), and be good citizens by doing something special and showing compassion for Patrice's family (Essential 10).

The finished product was something we all appreciated and felt proud of. My class and I were able to transform a tragedy into one of the most touching and indelible moments. Through our collective creativity, we were able to process our pain, comfort his family, and honor our friend.

The Exercises

Linked to creativity, imagination is one of the highest functions of the human brain. While most people believe that a creative brain is the domain of a select "artistic" few, imagination and creativity are inherent qualities of every human brain that can be developed and strengthened through training. Brain Power exercises, including the ones that follow, aim to assist in such development.

LISTEN & DRAW

Materials:	Paper, writing implements, crayon/markers, music, music player.
When to use it:	Calming and centering, after lunch.
The goal/objective:	Students will connect with different forms of music and interpret what they hear visually through drawing.
Considers national standards:	Craft and structure, presentation of knowledge and ideas, conventions of standard English.

INSTRUCTIONS

1. Select two to three stylistically different pieces of instrumental music. For example, smooth jazz, classical, and vibrant percussion.

2. Have students sit comfortably with eyes closed, quietly listening to one of the songs.

3. Ask students: "What colors come to mind?" "Do you see any shapes?" "Can you feel certain emotions?"

4. Replay the musical piece, this time while students use colored writing implements that they feel match the music, to "draw" the music.

5. Encourage them to let their hands move freely in response to the music and create anything they want. (Some students may "doodle," while others create more traditional drawings.)

6. Repeat with one or two other musical selections.

7. Discussion: "What are the similarities and/ or differences in your results based on each piece?" "How did it feel to connect with the energy of the music?"

Extensions & modifications: Older students may choose to write in response to the music rather than draw.

💡 CREATIVE SHAPES

Materials:	Creative Shapes Worksheet (see Appendix), writing implements such as markers or crayons.
When to use it:	After lunch.
The goal/objective:	Students will create as many unique pictures as possible using the shapes from the worksheet provided.
Considers national standards:	Integration of knowledge and ideas, presentation of knowledge and ideas.

INSTRUCTIONS

1. Distribute the Creative Shapes Worksheet.

2. Designate five to ten minutes for students to turn the shapes into pictures (e.g., a triangle might become a party hat; a circle, a balloon; and a square, a house).

3. Invite students to share their pictures.

4. Discussion: "How many different drawings were you able to create from just one shape?" "How did you use your creativity in this activity?" "Which one is your favorite?"

Examples & modifications: To adapt into a group activity, divide students into small groups. Using a piece of chart paper or poster board, invite the group to collaborate on a group drawing using one shape of their choice.

CREATE-A-DANCE

When to use it:	Energizer, mood changer.
The goal/objective:	Students will work together to choreograph and perform a group dance.
Considers national standards:	Key ideas and details, comprehension and collaboration, vocabulary acquisition and use.
Note:	No music required.

INSTRUCTIONS

1. Divide students into small groups, no greater than six, if possible.

2. Each group picks one of the ten Brain Power Essentials and creates a dance that interprets or embodies that Essential. Note: This can be done with or without music.

3. For inspiration, the groups should draw from other Brain Power exercises, movements, and activities.

4. Set a time limit to create the dance, and ask each group to perform.

Extensions & modifications: Play a simple beat or light instrumental track to help students through the choreography. Depending on the level of the group, the students can work as different units to create several dance sequences based on one Essential topic and combine them for a class dance. Invite students to create a class song about their agreed-upon Essential, and choreograph a group dance to go with it.

Character

Kindness in words creates confidence. Kindness in thinking creates profoundness. Kindness in giving creates love.
– Lao Tzu

What is character exactly? American biologist, naturalist, and author E.O. Wilson asserts that character is the "internalization of the moral principles of a society." Data analysis conducted by the Collaborative for Academic, Social, and Emotional Learning (CASEL) showed that students who receive instruction in "social and emotional learning" about such moral principles had more positive attitudes about school and improved an average of eleven percentile points on standardized achievement tests, compared to students who didn't receive such instruction.

Moral principles are pre-wired in the brain, according to neuroscience, and we naturally know how to get along. The traits that are part of our biology might be reinforced or manifested in different ways, but character is not the same as behaviors. Character consists of overarching principles that are universal across cultures. The principles can include basic human traits such as honesty, integrity, responsibility, and empathy.

Character development helps students become better communicators, productive and integral members of a team, efficient leaders, and proactive members of their communities. Because of the unique circumstances and precarious age groups of many students, they are often not yet connected to their inner character, or are unable to define it, and therefore drift from the ability to set goals for themselves and see how their lives can purposefully intertwine with the lives of others, their communities, and beyond.

Brain Education aims to mend this disconnect between students and self-awareness and identity. For instance, by helping students focus on the dreams they have in their hearts through an activity called I Have a Dream, Brain Power empowers them to see themselves as important leaders. Other activities stand to pull the latent leadership out of students, often to their own surprise.

Jeffrey was a tall, handsome eighth grader at Middle School 29X who had been placed in our leadership program for at-risk junior high school students in the South Bronx's District 7. Jeffrey had been held back a year for failing grades. He also had trouble controlling his anger and had been suspended from school several times for fighting with other students and assaulting a teacher. When he came to our first Brain Power elective class, Jeffrey said, "We're here cuz we're the bad kids, right? Are we the dumb kids, or what?"

The other students laughed in tacit agreement. I looked in Jeffrey's eyes and could see years of pain beneath his veneer. I surveyed the twelve students, making eye contact with each of them as I spoke: "You are here because someone—your teacher, guidance counselor, or principal—has identified you as having leadership potential. This does not mean you are the best student in your class; it means other kids in your class listen to what you say. Now, that doesn't mean you are necessarily leading your peers in a positive direction right now, but the purpose of this program is to build a group of confident, positive leaders who can help change the school's culture. You will need to follow rules and work hard. If that's something you want to do, please stay. If not, the door is right there."

I spoke with strength, because I knew if these teenagers didn't fully commit, the program wouldn't work. But mixed with strength was sincerity that told the students that they were there for a good reason, and I truly believed they were worth it. I could tell Jeffrey trusted me, because he never took his eyes off me as I spoke from my soapbox. After my speech, Jeffrey's demeanor changed: he sat up straight, looked back at me respectfully, and said one word, "Cool."

We taught several weeks of Brain Power classes at Jeffrey's school, focusing on team building, physical exercises to build strength and perseverance, and meditation to create inner focus. Then we had a two-day empowerment program. Held in the gym, sixty at-risk students from two neighboring junior high schools spent the entire day challenging themselves through fun and transformative activities. This is not to say I didn't receive resistance, which reared its head during the Bridge Game. In this game, students have to cross a walkway created by two parallel lines of teachers and students, which we refer to as a bridge. There are two rules:

1. Do your best.
2. Cross the bridge creatively. Don't copy others; find your own way.

After explaining the rules and showing a demo, the majority of the kids sat down, refusing to allow themselves to look silly, too afraid of others' judgment to try. I spoke to the group about leadership and its connection to taking risks, reminding them that we've created a safe space, free of judgment. They weren't having it. Then, my eyes set on Jeffrey's. He tried to look away at first, but then accepted my gaze.

"Alright, y'all. Let's do this," Jeffrey said, hopping up from his seated position. "I'm going first. Who's with me?" The other boys begrudgingly followed until everyone was on their feet. Jeffrey was the first to cross the bridge, and because of his example, the others did their best and completed the activity. Student sharing afterward was profound. Almost every one of the students said the same thing: they wanted to go across the bridge, but were too afraid of what other people would say. Because of Jeffrey's leadership, everyone learned not to be followers; they learned to be vulnerable; and they learned to trust themselves, stay focused, and not be afraid of judgment. It was a turning point, after which the group was able to participate in subsequent sessions that guided them to go deep inside themselves, reflect honestly on their lives, and set clear goals for their futures.

I thanked Jeffrey for his leadership, put my arm around his shoulder, and asked how it felt to help the other students overcome their fear and participate in the Bridge Game. "It feels good, man," he said. "It just feels good."

The Exercises

With an emphasis on goal setting, personal development, and a focus on the connection between strong character and success, the following activities inspire students to maximize their complete academic and social potential and exceed their own expectations.

👍 COMPLIMENT GAME

Materials (Optional):	An item that can be held easily, like a small rubber ball or stuffed animal.
When to use it:	Mood changer.
The goal/objective:	Students will identify and articulate sincere compliments for themselves and their classmates.
Considers national standards:	Convention of standard English, knowledge of language, communication and collaboration, information literacy, leadership and responsibility.

INSTRUCTIONS

1. Introduce an item (e.g., tennis ball, or anything that can be easily held and passed around) as a "talking symbol."

2. The teacher goes first, holding the talking symbol and giving himself or herself a sincere compliment.

3. The teacher will then pass the talking symbol to the next student while giving that student a compliment.

4. The student then gives himself or herself a compliment, and while passing the talking symbol to the next student, compliments that student. Students should only pass the talking symbol to those students who haven't had a turn.

5. Continue this pattern: students giving themselves a compliment and then passing a compliment to another classmate as they pass the talking symbol, until all students have had a turn.

Extensions & modifications: You might choose to begin with students giving compliments to the student to their right, and wait until students are more comfortable before introducing the option of complimenting themselves. Additionally, examples of compliments might need to be demonstrated before the activity begins. As per the "Three to One Praise" tip on page 70, encourage students to give character-based compliments about effort, choices, and actions, rather than topics like beauty, clothing, or possessions.

👍 I HAVE A DREAM

Materials:	Paper, writing implements, crayons/markers, if available.
When to use it:	Developing leadership.
The goal/objective:	Students will envision their life's dream and visualize the steps they need to take to actualize this dream.
Considers national standards:	Responsible behavior, respect for others, communication and collaboration, information literacy, social and cross-cultural skills.

INSTRUCTIONS

1. Brainstorm people who students believe followed their dreams. Encourage the group to include people from their everyday lives, as well as historical figures, modern personalities—anyone with whom they connect.

2. As the group offers examples, have someone write them on the board or on chart paper.

3. Identify not only the dream these people followed, but the steps they took to be successful and how their doing so helped others.

4. Have the students sit in good posture and form an Energy Ball (see Essential 4: Mindfulness). After they are

focused, guide them to open their BrainScreens and ask, "What is my dream?" "What am I doing to make this dream come true?" "Who is helping me?" "How does this dream benefit others?" Guide students to envision themselves working toward actualizing this dream in reality.

5. After their meditation, students reflect on their dream and create a drawing of themselves achieving that dream, including what they accomplished, who they helped, and what steps they took to be successful.

6. Invite students to share their work aloud.

7. Discussion: "How do you feel as you visualize this dream coming true?" "What do you want to be?" "What makes you happy?" "How can you make it all happen?"

Extensions & modifications: If time is limited, or students do not wish to draw, ask them to create a graphic web organizer to illustrate their dreams and how they will achieve them. The nucleus will represent their dream and branches can represent goals or actions to take to attain the dream. Older students can also integrate a creative writing exercise to further explain what the picture or web illustrates. Additionally, if students are not comfortable drawing, cutting images from magazines and newspapers to create a vision board can be inspiring and fun.

👍 VISION TREE

Materials:	Vision Tree template (see Appendix), writing implements, markers, crayons.
When to use it:	Developing leadership.
The goal/objective:	Students will compartmentalize their goals in order to set and meet larger, big-picture goals.
Considers national standards:	Range of reading and level of text complexity, comprehension and collaboration, information literacy, leadership and responsibility.

INSTRUCTIONS

1. Distribute copies of the Vision Tree template.

2. Explain that the tree is a symbol of the student's whole self, with the trunk representing their character and their essence, their innate parts that never change. The "branches" represent extensions of their life, parts of themselves, such as family, school, friends, while the "leaves" represent goals for those branches of their life. For instance, a leaf on the branch of "school," might be to improve in reading.

3. Students put to use their personality and imagination to complete the tree, writing goals into the leaves of their branches.

4. Encourage students to add color, flare, and creativity to their trees.

5. Exhibit Vision Trees in a designated space in the room, allowing time for the students to enjoy one another's work as if they were in an art gallery.

6. Discussion: "What steps will you take to reach or implement your goals?" "What are the similarities or differences between your classmates' goals and branches?" "Do you plan to choose to work on one branch first over another branch? Why? How will this help you stay true to your trunk, yourself?"

Extensions & modifications: If time or space does not allow for an exhibit, invite students to share one goal aloud for one of their branches. The activity can also be conducted at a group level. Draw the tree on chart paper and have the branches represent class rules and/or expectations. Students can write on leaves cut from construction paper their goal or step for how they will adhere to the rule or reach expectations of the class, and then attach them to the class tree.

Citizenship

We are Earth Citizens. We are the ones who have to save the earth, and our superpowers lie in our brains, waiting to be activated.
– Ilchi Lee

Brain Education takes a global approach to citizenship. By establishing the earth as the common foundation for our lives and encouraging a heightened awareness of, and appreciation for, the earth, students feel a natural responsibility to become "Earth Citizens" who contribute positively to their environment. By taking this perspective, students also feel a natural human connection that transcends nationality, race, religion, or gender.

A strong sense of citizenship improves academic performance, because it gives students the self-confidence and perspective to deal with everyday life occurrences, including interpersonal conflicts during recess, a disagreement in class, or sharing with others. They discover their voices and are given the tools to use their voices for good in their school, community, and society.

Early in my teaching career, I wanted to develop altruism and compassion in my students while exploring the concept of global citizenship, so I began a fundraiser called "Kids Helping Kids." The fundraiser involved helping the Malawi Children's Village, an orphanage for children in the southeastern African country who had lost one or both of their parents to AIDS. It was also an opportunity for my students to learn about Malawi, HIV/AIDS, and how to help those in need. In short, the project helped my fifth graders build a perspective that reached outside their own societal walls and contributed to the betterment of the larger world. Although my students were themselves from the projects and didn't have much, it was touching to see them saving their allowance to donate to children their age half a world away.

What I had hoped for most in this exercise of citizenship—caring about others in the world with an understanding that we are all connected—was brought to life on a class field trip when one of my students, Patrice, gave up his seat on the subway for an elderly man. In return, the man gave Patrice two dollars for "being a good kid." Remembering our fundraiser, Patrice, instead of spending the money on himself, donated it to the Malawian orphanage. Through his selflessness, our class learned that Patrice's citizenship on a Brooklyn subway caused a ripple effect that reached children on another continent. The lesson became a focus in our class: Even the smallest actions can have tremendous impact, and we all, no matter how much or how little we have, possess the power to effect change.

The Exercises

It has been my experience that most students don't need to be prompted to make a positive contribution to the world they live in, because they are innately eager to make a difference. Offering citizenship activities as an Essential of Brain Power enables them to know how to go about doing so, while preparing them for the realities of the adult world.

🏳 BRAIN DECLARATION

When to use it:	Mood changer, developing leadership.
The goal/objective:	Students will evaluate, interpret, and apply the Brain Declaration to their lives; they will create a sixth declaration that speaks to them.
Considers national standards:	Range of reading and level of text complexity, vocabulary acquisition and use.

BRAIN DECLARATION

First drafted at the Humanity Conference in Seoul, South Korea in 2002, the Brain Declaration is an inspirational set of ideas designed to help us become more confident, hopeful, and proactive. It describes all of the characteristics of a Power Brain. Making the Brain Declaration means recognizing and choosing the brain's fullest potential.

- **I declare that I am the master of my brain.**
  Translation: My primary intention is to maximize my brain's power.

- **I declare that my brain has infinite possibilities and creative potential.**
  Translation: With hundreds of trillions of potential neural connections, I recognize that through diligent practice, I can improve my abilities and live up to my true potential.

- **I declare that my brain has the right to accept or refuse any information and knowledge that it is offered.**
  Translation: Information is food for my brain; therefore, I must diligently manage the information that I internalize about myself and my surroundings. I possess the power of choice.

- **I declare that my brain loves humanity and the earth.**
  Translation: Cultivating a sense of leadership, community, altruism, and citizenship is an important component of healthy development.

- **I declare that my brain desires peace.**
  Translation: Proactively managing stress and emotions to create a harmonious relationship with myself and those around me helps me become a leader with strong character.

INSTRUCTIONS

1. Distribute copies of the Brain Declaration without translation points (see Appendix).

2. The class should read it out loud in unison several times.

3. Discussion: "What do you think of this declaration?" "Do you think it makes sense or applies to you? Why or why not?" "Which line is your favorite? Why?"

4. Invite students to personalize this declaration by adding one line to their copy.

5. Students take turns reading the declaration to the rest of the class, along with their addition.

Extensions & modifications: For younger students, post the Brain Declaration on a bulletin board or display it on an oversized easel. Talk about each line and decide as a class what line to add that would help the students as a community, rather than individualizing the declaration. Each student can sign the declaration in solidarity. Older students can memorize the declaration and recite it at the beginning of each day to set a positive tone.

EARTH CHALLENGES & SOLUTIONS

Materials (Optional):	Earth Challenges & Solutions Worksheet (see Appendix).
When to use it:	Developing leadership.
The goal/objective:	Students identify problems the earth is facing, raise awareness, and brainstorm solutions.
Considers national standards:	Fluency production and distribution of writing, analysis, inquiry, and design.

INSTRUCTIONS

1. Discuss some challenges threatening the earth (e.g., pollution, global warming, limited water supply or other resources, etc.).

2. Write each challenge on a board or chart paper.

3. Brainstorm with the students some solutions to each challenge, and write them down.

4. For each solution, brainstorm ways people can implement each solution, asking, "Of the challeng-

es listed, what could we do right now to help to begin to solve the problem?" "What can we do at school? At home? As individuals? As a group?" "How will these ideas make a positive impact on the issues the earth faces?"

Extensions & modifications: Older or more advanced students may brainstorm and write down many answers in response to the prompts. They can then use their brainstorm to write a poem, paragraph, or journalistic article sharing their thoughts and ideas.

ALTRUISTIC ACTIONS

When to use it:	Mood changer, developing leadership.
The goal/objective:	Students will brainstorm actions that benefit others.
Considers national standards:	Integration of knowledge and ideas; comprehension and collaboration; analysis, inquiry, and design.

INSTRUCTIONS

1. Offer a definition and examples of altruism.
   - *Chores:* Without being asked first, do a chore around the house.
   - *Reach Out:* Talk to someone at school who seems lonely.
   - *Compliments:* Sincerely compliment someone in your family or community.
   - *Appreciation:* Tell friends or family members something you appreciate about them.
   - *Grow Something:* Plant a flower, fruit, or vegetable.
   - *Share:* Teach someone something you have learned in Brain Power.
   - *Clean:* Pick up litter or trash around school, home, or the neighborhood.

2. Brainstorm other examples of altruistic actions.

3. Ask each student to choose and commit to completing at least one altruistic action in the next twenty-four hours.

4. The next day, invite students to share their experiences and reactions, as well as other people's responses toward their altruistic actions.

Extensions & modifications: Students may want to create a plan for completing a certain number of altruistic actions over a certain length of time. They can report their progress, their feelings after completion, and ideas for how to integrate altruism into their daily lives.

Resources

Body & Brain Checkup Chart

Record the number of points after each exercise.

STRETCHING . . . . ◯

1 point   Fingers do not touch the floor.
2 points Fingertips touch the floor.
3 points Palms touch the floor.

WRIST TWIST . . . . ◯

1 point   I cannot straighten my arms out.
2 points I can straighten my arms out,
              but it's painful.
3 points I can easily straighten my arms.

BALANCE CHECK . . . . ◯

1 point   I have a hard time balancing
              for 10 seconds.
2 points I can balance with my eyes open,
              but not closed.
3 points I can balance well with my eyes open
              or closed.

STRENGTH CHECK I . . . . ⬤

1 point   I can hold the posture for more than 30 seconds.

2 points I can hold the posture more than 1 minute.

3 points I can hold the posture for more than 2 minutes.

STRENGTH CHECK II . . . ⬤

1 point   Less than 10 squats

2 points 10-20 squats

3 points 20-30 squats
                (*add 1 point for each
                additional 10)

ENDURANCE CHECK . . . ⬤

1 point   Less than 3 minutes

2 points 3–6 minutes

3 points More than 6 minutes
                (*add 1 point for each
                additional minute)

Great Job! Add up your points and write the total in the box.

TOTAL . . . . ⬤

Emotions List

Write your response to each exercise.

1. Give an example of when you feel the following emotions. For instance, you feel happy when you play with your friends.

EMOTION	EXAMPLE
Happy	
Sad	
Angry	
Surprised	
Scared	
Excited	
Worried	
Love	
Peaceful	

2. Make a list of the different emotions you have felt today.

HSP Smile Picture

Earth Challenges & Solutions

1. List some problems that the earth is facing right now.

2. Think of a solution for each problem.

PROBLEM   **SOLUTION**

Push-up Progress Chart

DATE:	DATE:	DATE:
TODAY'S PUSH-UPS:	TODAY'S PUSH-UPS:	TODAY'S PUSH-UPS:
DATE:	DATE:	DATE:
TODAY'S PUSH-UPS:	TODAY'S PUSH-UPS:	TODAY'S PUSH-UPS:
DATE:	DATE:	DATE:
TODAY'S PUSH-UPS:	TODAY'S PUSH-UPS:	TODAY'S PUSH-UPS:

Creative Shapes

Create as many pictures as possible using the shapes below.

Brain Declaration

1. I declare that I am the master of my brain.

2. I declare that my brain has infinite possibilities and creative potential.

3. I declare that my brain has the right to accept or refuse any information and knowledge that it is offered.

4. I declare that my brain loves humanity and the earth.

5. I declare that my brain desires peace.

Speed Brain

SPEED BRAIN TEST 1

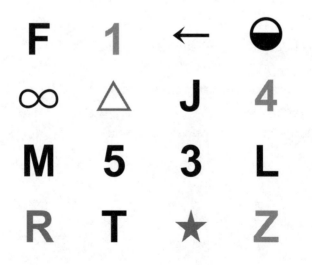

SPEED BRAIN TEST 2

Vision Tree

Brain Power Wellness Programs

Brain Power Wellness programs use an exciting combination of physical, emotional, and cognitive exercises to tap into your infinite brain potential. Its programs empower children and adults to improve their focus, confidence, memory, creativity, and emotional wellness while reducing stress and anxiety.

For Kids: Our classes and leadership programs empower kids ages 4–16 to maximize their brain potential.

For Schools: We've worked with thousands of students (Pre-K–12), teachers, and parents in over 400 schools in the U.S.

For Adults: Brain Power classes and empowerment workshops teach relaxation and mindfulness to create optimal life balance.

For Families: Our Family Classes and Family Retreats bring health and happiness to the whole family.

To find out about Brain Power Wellness programs and workshops in your area or to order classroom posters, please visit **BrainPowerWellness.com** or email **admin@ BrainPowerWellness.com**.

Acknowledgments

I would like to extend my sincere gratitude to the staff of Best Life Media, especially Jiyoung Oh and Michela Mangiaracina, for their editorial support. To Peter Hornung, who walked and talked with me for hours, listening to all my stories and helping transcribe and organize the book's content.

To Michele Matrisciani for her editing and supporting writing expertise. To Christina Neubrand who helped write up many of the exercises in Part 2. To Wayne Purdin for his help proofreading. To Ivan Cuadros for his lifelike illustrations. To Kiryl Lysenka for his neat design and to Teejay Luna for additional design support.

To Ilchi Lee, for creating Brain Education System Training and inspiring millions worldwide and for helping me realize my value. To Nora for her mentorship over the past ten years. To our amazing Brain Power team: Laura Castagnino, Katie Brisley-Logue, LaToya Morgan, Peter Hornung, Dianne Jerome, Lioubov Zozoulia, Cathy Martinez, Alina Pikula, Jessica Thiel and Jonelle Moore and to our international network of Brain Power Wellness trainers, instructors, mentors, and leaders: Your work is sacred and infinitely meaningful. Let's change the world one child at a time.

About the Author

Dave Beal is the Program Director and Head National Trainer for Brain Power Wellness. His specialty is in training educators, administrators, parents, and students on how to use their brain potential to its fullest through Brain Education. Over the past nine years, Dave has collaborated with  400 schools—training 12,000 teachers and 50,000 students.

Dave holds a B.A. from the University of North Carolina at Chapel Hill and a Masters in Education from Pace University in New York. He got involved in Brain Education when he was a teacher in the New York City Public School system and used these mind-body methods to transform his classroom during his time teaching in Brooklyn and Freeport, Long Island.

Dave has led experiential Brain Education sessions and lectures at the United Nations Headquarters, Nike Corporate Headquarters, and the University of Brain Education in South Korea. He has also presented Brain Education to the Congress of New Mexico, and has received praise and support from the NYC Schools Chancellor for his work in helping improve social emotional wellness throughout New York City.

His vision is to help every school in the U.S. become a "Brain Power School" that promotes health, happiness, peace, and optimal achievement for each member of the school community. He lives in Long Island with his wife and son. For more information about Dave's work, visit BrainPowerWellness.com.

Other Books from Best Life Media

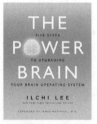

The Power Brain
Five Steps to Upgrading Your
Brain Operating System
By Ilchi Lee | *$19.95*
A user's manual for your remarkable brain.
With a five-step approach to a Power Brain,
learn how to use your brain to discover your
value, recreate the story of your life, and claim
a new destiny.

Principles of Brain Management
A Practical Approach to Making
the Most of Your Brain
By Ilchi Lee | *$13.95*
Drawing from his world-renowned Brain Education method, Ilchi Lee provides readers simple techniques to release the brain's creative
and cognitive potential.

Brain Wave Vibration
Getting Back into the Rhythm of
a Happy, Healthy Life
By Ilchi Lee | *$14.95*
Learn how to move your body to your own
internal, natural healing rhythms in order to
slow down your brain waves and unleash your
body's own innate healing ability.